Working Miracles

Simeon Kayiwa

*You too can receive miracles
on earth today!*

New Wine Press

New Wine Press
PO Box 17
Chichester
England PO20 6YB

ISBN: 1 903725 24 0

Typeset by CRB Associates, Reepham, Norfolk
Printed in England by Clays Ltd, St Ives plc

Dedication

To my lovely wife Celia

Contents

Acknowledgements

Your Excellency, Y.K. Museveni, President of the Republic of Uganda, the words 'I encourage you to do the work of God' you wrote in our visitors book when you laid the foundation stone on the Namirembe Christian Fellowship building are a source of great encouragement and motivation to me and my ministry in Uganda and around the world. Your Excellency, I gratefully acknowledge your support in this, my first book.

Your Majesty, the King of Buganda, Ronald Muwenda Mutebi, I greatly appreciate your encouragement to me and my ministry. On several occasions I have met you at your palace and recall most thankfully the great work done by your grandfather King Muteesa I in receiving God into our nation.

Thank you, Celia, for your encouraging me by provoking me to write this book.

Thank you, Barbara, my secretary for your dedication and commitment.

Thank you, Alan, for typing well into the night.

Thank you, Kay and Andrew Gill, for your support during this project.

Thank you Dad, Yosiya, for the price you and mum, Erivada, paid for my future that you had no idea about.

God deeply bless all the names mentioned above.

Amen

Simeon Kayiwa

Foreword

In this 21st century there is a growing hunger for spirituality, a spirituality which is both real and inspiring. No doubt it was just the same at the time of Christ. The people of Israel were almost asleep; and then a prophetic and powerful move came, as if from nowhere. With the perplexity of the nation of Israel overrun with Romans and underinspired by its spiritual leaders – there came the voice of one crying in the wilderness. A way would be opened up, and even greater surprises would follow.

After John – who was himself surprised at what followed – there came another - full of grace and truth. The truth was challenging, fresh, with new angles on old belief systems. The grace was amazing, supernatural, expressing power beyond the imagination of almost everyone. Jesus came – lived outside the box, and did miracles which were a catalyst to faith or rejection. He was for the falling and rising of many.

And so God has done such things over the centuries, raising up new, bright shining lights which penetrate the darkness. People who see such ministries can be excited and filled with a sense of privilege, or they may be offended and develop a mindset of criticism. In Uganda, in the midst of perplexity and consternation, God has raised up several amazing ministries – bright lights shining in the universe of complex and fallen mankind. Simeon Kayiwa is one such ministry, a son of a Baganda warrior – but also much more!

Read the book – but suspend your disbelief. It is not fiction, but it is not reality as most of us know it. Simeon is a man of intellect and education – not a simple, ill-educated person to be relegated in some way, to be ignored or ridiculed. No, here is a man of revelation and conviction, who has lived faith, experienced the heavenlies, and seen God's power let loose on earth.

Yes, read the book – but beware! It is not fiction, it is a challenge, a potential offence, and a potential inspiration. You will not be able to avoid the challenges – to ask, to believe, to receive.

I have known Simeon for a number of years. I have heard of his anointing and been uplifted. Better still, I have met the man, along with his wife Celia, and his children. I have seen the church at Namirembe Christian Fellowship – and I see good fruit. (I have also seen the mango tree that you will read of!) He leads a vibrant community of faith and power – a place of safety and honesty, a place where Jesus Christ is honoured and worshipped.

Let the real life story fill your life with thanksgiving, that God is still at work in the lives of those yielded to Him, at work in places where evil has held sway and damaged many lives and generations. What God has begun in Uganda is good news for its people, but He has not finished yet. There is so much more healing and grace to flow in that nation, and out from it to the ends of the earth. As you read, who knows what blessings will flow to you? For everything is possible when you believe.

Tony Morton
Cornerstone Network
Southampton, UK
June 2003

Introduction

A miracle is a supernatural event. When it happens, any ordinary person would realise here is something extraordinary. 'I had better take notice of this, maybe there is an intelligence out there I have not been aware of before, I should investigate this further. Maybe I could get to know the intelligence responsible for this,' he or she would think.

Because there have been many miraculous instances documented, in my own experience, in the lives of other God-fearing people today and written about in the Bible, it is important for you to read a book such as this.

Knowledge changes people. Often it changes people for the better. A positive attitude to these things can have direct benefit to you and your family in the affairs of daily living. Please take a little while to read this book and carefully consider its implications for your life. You stand to benefit greatly by this knowledge. Applying the same principles to your own life and understanding the same revelation as me, that you read about in *Working Miracles*, will strengthen your faith and reveal God to your heart.

In your everyday struggle, you will receive comfort, vision and strength to live a life pleasing to God.

Applying your knowledge with faith can transform even bitter and difficult circumstances and will help restore much desired balance to your mind in such a way as to restore peace.

All the stories in this book are true. They really happened.

They show that it's not just the great men and women of faith recorded long ago in the Bible, but similar extraordinary miracles can and do happen to ordinary people in our time.

I am so very glad that you are about to give me your time and attention to inspire you to engage in these most important matters of the supernatural realm which surrounds us, if only you have eyes to see it.

Chapter 1

Where it All Began

First of all, it's a miracle I am writing this book. Slightly over twenty years ago you would not have enjoyed my response had you mentioned the word 'God' in my ears! I would have done all I could to frustrate and enrage you. I was a typical example of a spoilt lad to whom God in his mercy demonstrated His renowned patience in permitting my sin to go unpunished for a long time.

My Christian parents endured many onslaughts from me as I used the Word of God, sweet music to their ears, to attack them as I grew up. They revered the Bible as a central part of their lives, but to me it lacked relevance, meaning or vital power. There seemed to be nothing of healing, nothing of blessing and nothing so great about this Word. In addition I had to endure the invasion of my home by a constant stream of strangers who seemed to me to be taking advantage of my parents' beliefs and generosity, particularly as we were not rich ourselves, to selfishly obtain their own comfort at our expense.

Frankly speaking, during my teenage years, a heaven-promised survival of human beings sounded a far-fetched implausible myth to me. I could not buy into that. If God really existed, I thought, He might just have made Uganda and other happier places to live in on the same day, but it made no sense to me all the while many hopelessly wounded people were dying daily on our streets. While people in other countries enjoyed their lives, I witnessed many perishing through neglect. In our hospitals unattended patients remained doubled up in agony awaiting release into future bliss. Ours was a story of a humanity that had lost its fight for survival, all hopes dashed ... have you heard of Idi Amin? Then you will understand what I mean.

Why, I thought, should anyone in the church or mosque settle for a mere lullaby? It was time to put the toys away, no time for playing games. Men, women and children were being slaughtered like cattle and infants raped. Spirits were ruthlessly crushed. How could anyone trust in a distant hope for the future? In the face of a dictatorial regime's habitual murder of innocents, how could people believe in a God who has real authority on earth? If Idi Amin was able to murder the country's archbishop, demonstrating his defeat of heaven's own church, how almighty was God? The contrast of the vast numbers of perishing humanity being soothed by thoughts of one individual's distant death on a cross looked to me like a preacher's wishful fantasy. It seemed like sensational mishmash. Just because we were so desperate was no reason to be foolishly gullible. A real solution to the problem was needed, not a post-dated, religious cheque, or we were going to be wiped off the face of the earth.

King Fred of Buganda, Uganda's first president, had been overthrown by Obote, the Prime Minister eleven years previously. Civil war broke out. For strange reasons a false political dichotomy developed between the northern and southern parts of the country which were incited to armed clashes. As parts of the country were poised to tear each other to pieces, politicians sat back, boasting of their smart strategy for a better Uganda! No-one who, like my parents, had voted in the 1962 polls for Ugandan Independence would have believed that within a few years the country could decline to a state of war because of a succession of mismanagement, the breakdown of infrastructure, murders, abject poverty, disease and massive social despair. National destiny was being sacrificed on the altar of appeasement of the personal appetites of lucky politicians. At the start had been ordinary politics, but this turned slowly into mediocre battles of cartoon characters, and then slipped into a more sinister path of real knives and bullets, explosives, detentions without trial, exiles, dangerous military alliances and even influencing indirectly armed conflict between the superpowers. In the end, throughout the country, bleeding city after bleeding city cried out to heaven day after day, without any seeming evidence of an answer being thrown out of the window from God. Time without end the cries of the perishing went without response. Hands continued to beg earnestly for mercy. Except mine. I had long since given up faith in God.

Out of this extremely hot melting pot jumped the politically hungry Idi Amin, wielding a loaded gun. He overthrew Prime Minister Obote, splashing himself liberally with military medals, and travelled the length and breadth of the country killing indiscriminately. Every time his opponents tried vigorously to stop him, he murdered everyone in the vicinity at random. Every sense of civilisation drained away and hope was extinguished. Corruption in the government was sky high. Theft was even endemic in the army and no sensible means of running the country remained. Those who survived the hail of bullets were knifed down by poverty. Disease became impossible to treat due to malnutrition, lack of organisation and funds. A country once called the 'pearl of Africa' by Winston Churchill became the embarrassing eyesore of modern civilisation.

As a teenager I saw no place for myself in politics in Uganda. I felt lost, abandoned. I saw half-eaten corpses rotting openly in the street! I was appalled by the revolting scenes of struggles within the Amin regime. Many of my friends and I were very angry with Amin, but were even more enraged by the indifference of the rest of the world to our situation. No-one on earth or heaven seemed to care about us. Governments were even supplying more arms to Amin! The same governments were sending preachers of Islam and Christianity. Did they take us for fools? Did they think that just because we were not in power, mosques or churches, or in government ourselves that we were stupid? There was no recognition of the fact that people were dying.

Libya, France, the Soviet Union, the United States, Sudan, Egypt, China and Saudi Arabia continued trade links with Uganda. They are all members of the United Nations. How could they, under the principle of non-interference in the internal affairs of member countries, ignore the very safety and continuity of the human race on which nations depend, by continuing to trade with the Amin regime? To whom then could we go for safety? This policy of non-interference in the internal affairs of a country I thought was a conspiracy of wicked national leaders to promote their own survival at the expense of lesser mortals. If there was a God, He surely never intended fellow human beings to have such an inhuman attitude to others in pain.

I saw so many dead bodies that it would not have had any impact on me if someone had said, 'He died instead of you'. There was nothing significant about the death of a single human being at that time. If someone had told me that He died for me, I would have said, 'How did He come to know me? I don't recognise Him. I'm sorry, He should not have done such a passionate thing for my sake. Who am I anyway? Who cares about a suffering Ugandan?' The world outside called us a country forgotten by God. We were looked on by ordinary Kenyans and our own police force as the dirt of the world. Yet it was not we who were dirty. Not even the most clean-hearted of God's people was safe from Idi Amin's gunpowder. If the UN continued to support such regimes as this by their policy of non-interference in internal affairs of member states, then the author and finisher of life was Amin,

Bokasa, Doe, Hitler, Mobutu and the like. The grim reality was that my only chance of survival was money, a good education, or a good pair of legs with which to run away fast from the danger of an approaching soldier. Or on the other hand, living was enjoying the pleasure of a laugh and joke with friends, or the attraction of a beautiful girl.

When faced with our personal safety we had a number of difficult decisions to make. Should we defend ourselves, our children and loved ones and our property with guns? Should we join a group dedicated to the overthrow of the government and risk an accusation of treason? What should we do when faced with the sight of someone injured and probably dying in the street? Try to help or rush on quickly to avoid becoming a casualty? To arm myself with a firearm was unthinkable, but the cost of staying alive was to risk unpleasant alternatives. To expect a quick removal of this decadent regime was also too much to hope for. When I saw the speed with which sanity, sanitation, the sanctity of human life and civilisation were disappearing under the rule of the gun I was chilled to the bone. To walk the streets of the capital, Kampala, and see nothing but a general picture of decay, people suffering, languishing in a pool of their own blood as a result of capricious treatment from the hidden pistols of Idi Amin's men, was brutalising.

Faced with shops emptied of the necessities of life, roads full of potholes, buildings desperately needing repainting, no running water in our taps, children walking the streets without shoes, I became demoralised and cynical. I had no values, nothing to hold on to. I had been deeply hurt by bad girls. It felt as if my heart had been stabbed repeatedly. I thought there was nothing that could soothe my heartache. Everyone, everywhere seemed poised waiting to tear everyone limb from limb each hour we lived through the Amin era.

So I chose to find solace in dirty songs. My best friends at university were into a very debauched lifestyle. They would sing songs they had composed and sleep around. Everything in our lives denied the existence of God. I cherished the company of those closest friends who insisted on a highly immoral way of life in these years of growing up. It was useless to plan for a future. In this corrupt haze of songs of despair I started drinking heavily. What a contrast to my life as a preacher and writer of Christian songs now!

I am amazed when I think of what miracles God has done for me. I had no right to deserve the work that has been entrusted to me. It should have gone to someone else. I certainly did not deserve to be the holder of such a testimony to the grace of the Lord Jesus Christ!

In December 1977 something happened to me that, considering the opinion I so strongly held, should never have happened. After completing my studies I was working as a teacher in an Anglican Church school in Uganda. One morning as I woke up before starting my preparation for morning class, who do you think appeared to me? Standing and looking at me, He gave me, a stranger, the strangest feeling I have ever had. I trembled like a leaf. I was covered in goose pimples. I was overcome with a mixture of fear, astonishment, a strange feeling of inner turmoil and an unaccustomed loss of self-esteem. At the same time I was also very happy to be in the presence of this awesome Man, who I had considered dead nearly 2000 years before. Did I look sleepy? I must have done, because He said, 'Wake up! Read Isaiah 60. Go and bring My people back to Me. Tell them I am the greatest power in all heaven and earth. Tell them to leave witchcraft and come back to Me. I will be with you wherever you go, to perform miracles and wonders, by which people will know that I have sent you.'

My heart said 'yes', my mind said 'NO!'

I was not finished with the world yet. I had not finished living my own life. I was still a young man, barely out of my teens, and had no audience waiting to listen to me. At that time under Idi Amin it was illegal to be a born-again Christian and I did not want to join any of the religions that were allowed. Besides, in order to survive, they had to agree to being used as political tools by the regime. One example is that they would pray for Amin's government in every service, not for his downfall, but for his continued protection. The Moslems and only three other Christian denominations were permitted to worship. We nicknamed these organisations the 'gang of four'. The year before was when the Anglican archbishop, Janani Luwum, had been murdered. To my mind this had demonstrated God's lack of earthly power. Surely it would be impossible for a mere man to kill a representative of God's own Church? To be a member of that church would have felt like agreeing to bow before a defeated God. I had just heard that Jesus was the greatest power in all heaven and earth, but I still needed to see some concrete evidence of this said power on earth. To do what was asked, I was looking at something similar to the contest of Moses before Pharaoh that I had seen in a movie as a child. I reasoned that in order to function properly in Uganda, God had to act in a similar fashion with Idi Amin. Amin had bragged that he was the conqueror of the British Empire. By deciding to preach I was defying the Amin decree outright, just like Moses. I argued with God 'Lord, send someone else. Send the bishop, the cardinal, the Muslim sheik or the like. But who am I?' In addition I had run up large debts I could not repay, I had scandals to live down and needed to sort out my immoral ways. I had no support team, no platform, no programme and was unknown by any important names.

I could not preach without first sorting these things out. I was used to running away to avoid unpleasantness. How could that change? I would prefer to continue escaping the attention of approaching soldiers by running on, running away, hiding under my bed, in the dog or chicken house. Especially we would need to keep away from the attention of the secret police that were everywhere, informing on every-one. Running was a common way of life for most people, not just me. We were all witch hunted, doomed, a nation on the run, shadowed daily by Idi Amin's secret police. I did not want to preach, only to run. My daily life was hiding from soldiers, and those I owed money to. There was no way I could avoid infuriating Idi Amin one way or another if I preached, even if I succeeded in evading the decree which banned speaking outside the premises of the gang of four. Humanly I decided it was impossible to obey Jesus. I would wait until I had a demonstration of God's almighty power. It's amazing how many thoughts can go through your mind in a very short time. To all of this Jesus just said, 'I know, but go!'

Oh! So I would go after all. Who was I not to obey? But to whom should I go? I supposed I would start with small children. How would I start? How do I introduce the subject of God to people? What sort of a preacher should I be? I didn't like many of the silly things I had seen people do such as telling unconcerned members of the public about their past sins and failures. I did not like street screaming.

After my mother died in 1973, in spite of much prayer, I was convinced Jesus was not one of my friends. I certainly had many hang-ups to overcome, didn't I? Satan had really tied my thinking up with many dark thought patterns. Today, when I walk down memory lane with Jesus, I laugh as I remember how I wriggled out of Satan's grasp. When I stand in front of crowds of tens of thousands, it's amusing to remember how it all began. When I see how many lives are changed I laugh with enjoyment. Let's laugh. God laughs also at Satan's works. *'The Lord laughs at him, for He sees his day is coming'* (Psalm 37:13).

It takes some time before other people are convinced of your change of heart. On the basis of reputation, even though they have been told of your conversion to Christ, parents are inclined to warn their daughters not to marry someone they regard as unproven. Celia's parents and acquaintances were no exception. She was inundated with conflicting advice as to whether she should marry nineteen years ago. Some, although knowing that in Christ one becomes a new creation, thought our marriage would be wrong. Sometimes those fears may be justified, I grant you. I am glad Celia believed firmly that the Simeon the world had known before was a different person from what I had become. She had confidence that a recrudescence of my past was ridiculous. It's wise to listen to people, but you do not have to believe everything you hear. If you don't rubbish the rumourmongers, you'll end up believing enough rubbish to turn you into a garbage pit yourself! Celia and I decided we would believe our promises to one another and on the 16th of May 1981, trusting Jesus who makes all things new, without fear walked down the aisle together as man and wife. It would be a futile exercise writing this book if God can't change us. It is my sincere hope that you will take the opportunity to change as you read about my experiences. I write with enormous gratitude to God for my deliverance from evil and for God's infinite love and mercy expressed to me in many ways.

As I sat in the teachers' common room deep in thought and prayer, my friend Robert sat down next to me drinking a cup of coffee. He tried to engage me in conversation. Every attempt he made was briefly, but humbly dismissed with a short answer. 'Yes. No. I don't know. I am not sure. Probably so, ask someone else.' He looked disappointed that I was unusually silent. Could it be that he was thinking it had something to do with the fact that he had so recently had the effrontery to challenge me over my recent conduct concerning the exam results of my pupils? I was rapt in thought. It was as though the promise of God was a big cheque in my hand. I had never seen anyone in my country that God had sent to do miracles. But so what? The promise of God had come to me, the 'vilest offender'. How marvellous that felt! My imagination was excitedly peering into the images of heaven and God's majesty that were filling the screen of my mind. I hardly noticed Robert's approach, I was so taken up with what I was seeing.

God uses His powerful oil to change our nature so that when we become new creatures we may do things beyond the natural ability of man. This is not just for fun. It is to give the world proof, because it is so full of argument. My whole nature changed that day. The world needs clear evidence. People need something punchy, something provocative, something crystal clear, something the world cannot do. The world needs something that walks upright, uprightly, like the walking, resurrected body of Lazarus. God's promise is like a huge store full of riches. Whatever promise you find in the Bible is no small matter. God is so mighty that it is the easiest thing for Him to fulfil any one of His promises. **When I sat in that teachers' common room in December 1977 at 10 a.m. I had nothing but a promise**.

It is my sincere hope that my experiences of life will give others like me in today's world an opportunity and encouragement to change as I have done, by the power of God. Things that should not have happened happened to me when Jesus came into my life. When we talk about Jesus we are reminding ourselves of Someone who does the impossible, the Lord who can deal with every inconvenient detail of our lives, be it biological, demonic, atavistic, or of an acquired nature. In these pages you have an opportunity to discover an entry into the premises of the Almighty in order to receive miracles. Jesus taught and proved that all things are possible if we believe.

Jesus is right. He has proved Himself to me in all ways, and not only to me but also to all I speak to that surely He is the Greatest Power in all heaven and earth. He calls me to contend with the world, with that same faith in the God of the prophets and apostles of old, who shut lions' mouths, raised the dead, healed dreaded diseases and did incredible signs and wonders. When miracles happen, His institution on earth will have respect instead of being downtrodden by the so-called wisdom of political rulers today. In the Bible the prophets never allowed God to be ridiculed by even such feared monarchs as Herod, Caesar, the Egyptian pharaoh, or the Babylonian dictator, Nebuchadnezzar. Unless we are serving a different God, how should we tolerate what our predecessors could not? 'No way, honey', as my American friends would say. Joking apart, I really am serious about this. I really do mean NO WAY! Many have tried to force me to shut up over the years. Old fogies have teamed up against me and made things pretty stark and gloomy. Society hates change. It often gets people really infuriated. Against all odds, by the grace of God, I have kept soldiering on. How can I stop when I have seen the things I have? The Almighty has subpoenaed me to appear in the witness box to give my evidence in defence of the unchallengeable truth that there is a God. I have to speak about the true experiences of the miracles I have seen.

In ignorance many people may contest the truth. They will continue to fight on. It is easy to fight a man, but when God turns a Man's name into an idea, before you know it, you end up attacking incredible numbers of people and their unseen source of strength. Paul was told by Jesus that that among the people he confronted by imprisoning believers, he had also been fighting Christ. There comes a time in every person's life when things get tough. At those times we need more than the ordinary to survive. We feel like running somewhere or to someone for safety. Our health, family situation, business or living situation can get so rough we need a refuge. Even when we do everything right, work very hard, eat the right food, speak the right language, pay our taxes, keep time, attend to all invitations and appointments, marry the right man or woman, wait patiently when we have to, go promptly when it is time to do so, drive at the correct speed and obey all the traffic regulations, still things can get dark and very rough indeed.

Wherever we go, therefore, it is important that evidence of God's power be produced. It will remind us, and the world, that Christ once thought of as dead and gone, but who was resurrected after three days, as promised before He died, is alive. Like Lazarus and Jesus, this proof makes a heaven promised survival of human beings not too highly improbable to buy into.

Anyway there I was, making my silent prayers of repentance. Robert's questions were as if someone was trying to interrupt a sweet telephone conversation. Eventually he left me alone. One by one my sins started to stagger away. Girls lost their beauty, cigarettes began to look demonic, and my man-made dreams of the future turned to lousy, empty shadows of life. Life began to wear a new look. With God, all things are possible. The oil of God was anointing me anew.

God was equipping me to become a brand new person. He was equipping me to live a victorious life. My old life was sagging with failures, shame and regrets. I was sad, lonely, depressed and confused. Life had put me down. The political relations between Kenya and Uganda had forced me to quit my job in Nairobi. I had gone there to study international law, international relations, psychology, and human physiology at university in Nairobi and now I was forced to leave. Kenya had become a very dangerous place for Ugandans. People from 'Amin's Country' were no longer welcome in Kenya. Unhappy circumstance followed on unhappy circumstance. Where was it all leading to? After the International University of Nairobi and Makerere University in Kampala I was qualified as an artist with 'a little bit plus' but that was not good enough for me. I was more ambitious than that. Even though my friends thought I was perfectly well educated enough, I felt empty. Truly I did not know what this emptiness was about. I did not know what purpose this emptiness was for. I did not realise it was not education I lacked; it was the oil of God. Because of my lack of oil my life had become a shambles. Mine was a sorry story of poverty, sadness, complaint, distress and dissatisfaction.

Chapter 2

The First Miracles

About a month before this amazing event, I had come back from a funeral some distance away to find all my belongings stolen. When I returned to school I found threats from a woman who was angry with me for neglecting her baby. She was demanding a DNA test to prove paternity. To tell you the truth I was not at all prepared to be there for the woman or her child. I was only sorry that she had believed me, and was sorry that I had got into a relationship with her. My legs were busy running from soldiers, now from a baby. I owed money besides. It was like a whole storm of evil had overtaken me. Unless the wind changed, I was in a lot of trouble. I badly needed a shift in wind direction. I needed help. I needed some intervention. I needed a force that could change all things in me and in my country.

Socially I was at that time head of the English and the Fine Arts departments of the school I was employed by. I was a respectable person. I was the youngest member of staff, yet held a head of department position. Some people would just call me 'mister', but when I called, they would come running to me shouting 'sir!' But inside I felt fragmented and injured by events. This was an inglorious chapter of our nation's history we were living in. There was no sir, or madam, none honour-able, no royalty in Amin's day. We were all a humiliated people.

My staff and I had only to the end of the week to hand in

our students' marked examination papers. As administrator it was my responsibility to see that the marks were awarded fairly and on time. The department was seriously short of staff so I had so many classes to mark. I had not a hope of doing this on time. To hit the deadline was impossible. It would have been like being given a deadline to drain the whole of Lake Victoria with a mere teaspoon. Even if I had worked all month with no sleep every night I would not have finished marking those papers. What was I to do?

I decided I would not even try to do it. Instead I listed all the students' names and at random I allocated them a result. I awarded them a stack of imaginary grades, failing some, passing a few and giving excellent results to others. Yet I couldn't even remember the faces of those students, whose names were in front of me, the students whose innocent future lay dangerously at the foot of my clumsy pen like necks of sheep. I then dumped their papers in the school garbage bin, and handed my results in. I did not see any need to be honest or act responsibly. I had no desire to be holy. The headmaster was delighted with the promptness of my results and even commended me to the other staff as a good example. I enjoyed his praise, yet in my heart I knew I was a liar. But that was the morality of the time. Survival, rather than righteousness, was the order of the day.

I had another problem. The school's security guard was short of fuel. He was responsible for burning the rubbish. He had a grudge against me. He didn't like the friendly overtures I had been making to his wife. Recently I had begun on occasions to share a joke or two with her. I thought he was a fool. And anyway I was not doing anything wrong. Even if I had, what could he do to me? His wife was very dirty, old, and insufferably ugly. Even a drunk teacher would be crazy to be attracted to her. But with the increasing number of accusations piling up against me in and around the school premises it was going to be difficult to silence crazy Alisando. It was going to be like disentangling myself from thorns or barbed wires no matter how insubstantial his accusation was going to be. To think that Alisando, the security guard, could believe and accuse me of making passes at his wife! That, I suppose, was the best day of her life, for her husband to publish such flattery about her. Their marriage must have taken a turn for the better! To pursue this act of kindness towards her, Alisando decided to pay me back with some of my own coin. First thing in the morning, as soon as the headmaster arrived, the headmaster received those unmarked papers in his hands from the security guard. What a sharp knife pierced my heart when the headmaster called me into his office. I couldn't believe what Alisando had done. I felt like hiring a gunman to hit him.

That week all the other teachers avoided me. One or two of the friendlier said, 'Come now, slow down Simeon. We all have our petty foibles. These things happen to everyone.' But they all knew I was going to be dismissed. 'I don't give a damn about being kicked out of this bloody job ...' After all, I bragged to myself, I had plenty of other fish to fry than being glued in this old fashioned den of grey-haired silly senior citizens. Poor headmaster! Even though he did have grey hair he was not at all a bad man even if I had no good words for him. In fact he forgave me when I apologised, and I even kept my job as head of the literature and fine arts department.

Although the headmaster forgave me, the students did not because they all had to sit the exams again. The teachers still discussed the business of Alisando's wife fervently. Especially one older man who had an eye on my privileged head of department position. None of this plotting had any effect until a consortium of well respected members of staff got together to move for my dismissal on the grounds of what they called my personality defects. Ironically it was because I had told the students that I had met Jesus and the staff accused me of trying to start a new religion. Others thought that my newfound interest in religion was only a front to cover for my recent examination paper scandal and other misdemeanours. The new religion allegation was indefensible to the headmaster since this was an Anglican Church school, so I was given until the end of term to pack my bags and leave. Students and teachers were told to stay away from me, especially to keep their distance from my new beliefs, which I had started to spread. Since my dismissal I have spoken to millions rather than just a few art and literature students.

Not everyone was convinced that to talk about faith in Jesus was a personality defect. Robert came to see me one day to ask for prayer. Robert taught Art and French in another school as well as in this school where we both were on staff. Even so, he did not think he was earning enough money to live on. 'If you really have seen Jesus, could you pray for me to get another job?' he asked. His 'if' had that same questioning tone as when Satan put the question to Jesus 'If you are the Son of God, turn these stones into bread.' It seemed to insinuate that I might not have met Jesus. What an unpleasant challenge. If I did not meet this challenge, he would remind me of a whole string of recent wrongdoing. He would bring up all my unsavoury past. Look at my young age. Look at my clothes, the same pair of cheap tired jeans I wore every day. And Robert was the one who criticised me the most over the examination paper scandal. So, as if to reciprocate the challenge, I said, 'Robert, that you may know that I did see Jesus, show me your resignation letter and I will show you the power of Jesus!' Robert did show me his letter of resignation. 'That you may know that I saw Jesus, next Tuesday go to Kampala City and stand by the main Post Office, any time you want, and you will meet someone there and he will offer you a job. You will be paid three times as much as you earn from these two schools where you earn currently.'

Later Robert told me he sensed something unusual about the new-religion business. He told his friends they would see something coming out of nothing. He stood outside the Post Office, at his own chosen time. He decided after waiting a while to go and see if there were any letters for him. So he opened his mailbox. As he did so, an old friend of his, not known by me, tapped him on the shoulder and said that the Greek Ambassador to Uganda had just asked him if he would like to take a job as general manager of his new company. The next day Robert was given an interview and offered a job as general manager. He was handed the keys of one of the best known, possibly the largest, shoe retailer in the city of Kampala at that time and given his own office. His salary was more than tripled, his house renovated at company expense and he also drove a company car to ease his personal transport needs. Robert rushed into the classroom of another school I taught at to tell me of his miracle. I was so sure I had heard Jesus that if Robert had not had his miracle, then my encounter with Jesus had not happened either. I would have called it a product of too vivid an imagination.

Robert needed no more convincing that there is a God in heaven. Tears rolled down his cheeks. 'Thank you, Simeon, I can see Jesus'.

'What else would you like Jesus to do for you?' I asked him a week later.

'I want to get married.' He replied.

'To who?'

'There was a girl called Robinah who I loved secretly nine years back.' But he had never told her of his feelings for her.

'Do you remember how you got your job? That you may get further convinced that I met Jesus, go to town next Tuesday and stop by the bus park any time of your choice. You will see Robinah there. Bring her to me. I will tell you to get married.'

Full of faith, Robert got dressed on the following Tuesday. I suppose the angels were also getting ready to give him the surprise of his life. He went down to the bus station and started looking at every girl he passed on the way. For a long time he looked around, behind him, to the left and right. All the time he was praising God, whose Word he carried in his hand in the form of the Good News Bible. It used to be my first Bible, which I had given to him as a present to remind him of the first miracle. At long last, late in the evening, he sat down on one of the benches at the central bus park. When he looked up again, Robinah, the secret desire of nine years, was sitting down on the same bench!

'Praise God, I've found you, Robinah', Robert thought. He told her how he had met Jesus after a brief conversation with a fellow teacher. About one week later he and Robinah were married. They had several children. Sadly Robert died only a year ago, while I was on a visit to Kenya. Robinah and their children are still in touch with me. The story of his life is still a mystery to them.

I have no special or significant background to be proud of. My ancestors consisted of only a very few Baganda warrior chiefs, who were surrounded by crowds of weaklings. My father's family emerged out of the murky gloom of rather uncertain, insecure genealogy in one of the lesser tribes of the Buganda people, the Kobe tribe. This genetic tree has only one or two major historical brave warriors. My grandfather changed his name in order to avoid being sent to war when our clan was called upon by the king. My mother was born to a shy, reclusive individual called Simeon and was brought up by her brother Aaron. Aaron was the only modern Buganda chief. I feared that I would be in many ways like my grandfather of the same name, who in his 83 years achieved almost total anonymity, except to influence an extremely small circle of friends. His life made little impact outside this close circle. Actually, in fact, I had become very like that Simeon. When the Lord called me I was a trembling, skinny, short, spineless weakling. I was five feet eight inches tall, had a tiny, thin body, weighing only 48 kilograms, I spoke with a pronounced stammer and had grown only the scantiest of moustaches in an attempt to boost my confidence.

My father was born casually, just like my aunt also. One day my grandmother went outside to see to her bananas in the garden when an idea suddenly popped into her mind to give birth. She quickly carried the idea out, there and then, by lying down on the ground in the banana patch. One, two three pushes and there we go. The baby was born. No baby clothes to hand, of course, so she wrapped him in a banana leaf. If a wandering dog had passed by at that moment it could have easily wolfed him down mistaking him for a piece of meat. Grandmother slept for some time after the birth. When she woke up luckily no such fate had befallen the child. In Uganda before the First World War, I think many children met such an end. I was born forty years later. At the time my dad was working as a teacher.

My mother was a peasant farmer. Before she died aged 49 in 1973 she raised a family of ten children. This was a very heavy burden, educating, feeding and clothing us all. Her only joy, when she would glow with pleasure, was when she would sing. She must have had quite some talent, because she was honoured by being buried in the Anglican churchyard. My father was an artist, but his ability did not rise to a significant level, so he was not considered worthwhile enough to merit the Anglican Church courtyard. On the contrary he was dismissed from the church when he refused to denounce what they considered my dangerous preaching and practise of faith in Jesus.

At the beginning of my life I expected that common sense, talent and academic torches would illuminate my way. But when the scales fell off my eyes and I saw Jesus, my whole outlook on life changed. There is no truer grace than when a miscreant such as I was is turned into a source of spiritual and moral light. When God illuminates an insignificant person's dark life through His Word, his life can be radically transformed. People may now find it hard to believe that these are the same lips that used to kiss prostitutes and cigarettes when I now powerfully speak God's Word with signs and wonders today. There is no truer grace than to hear a former stammerer make eloquent speeches worthy of loud applause. In my case it was essential that I should have started life in God's service as an outright, weak, stammering nonentity, so that now I can energetically attribute ALL my achievements solely to the power of God.

A person who is spiritually dead is not aware of this fact. He does not realise this. He lives a life in real danger and darkness, but until the light is turned on inside, he does not know it. I had acquired in my university days the darkest philosophy of life. When I studied psychology, art, literature, international law and so on, I was steeped in darkness. I learned that religion was 'the opium of the poor' as communists would say, but Jesus is surely a 'bright chap' as one socialist soldier calls Him in the book *Tortured for Christ*, by Richard Wurmbrand. Thank God, Jesus is not a religion, He is a Person.

By definition a miracle is not open to explanation by scientific enquiry. It is a deliberate contravention of the natural laws that govern the way our world functions. The occurrence of a miracle is deliberately intended to affirm that God's power is real. To a world polluted by proud science, logic and technology, Christianity makes no sense. Jesus said, *'Unless you people see signs and wonders, you will by no means believe'* (John 4:48).

When I began to work for the Lord, I started in great fear and trembling. I would shake like a leaf. But as time went on and I saw the many miracles that God was doing I became more confident that Jesus was with me. In fact, I became very firm and inwardly brave. Many weak, frightened people began to rely on me. They considered that I held the answer to many of our country's ills and indeed the country began to rely on me. Our nation, our institutions, and our people became frailer and frailer as Idi Amin's regime became even more determined to crush us under his wicked mortar fire. Body and spirit were smashed like china under the barrel of his gun. When Amin was challenged by guerrilla fighters, his ubiquitous detection monster was set loose on the public to shoot and kill anyone they chose under the pretext of clearing up any semblance or trace of opposition. We definitely needed a miracle or soon we were all dead men and women!

I spent many hours praying that Idi Amin would repent and turn to Jesus before it was too late. One day, in December 1978, after praying for a long time for him to save his soul from eternal loss, I fell asleep. During the night an angel told me not to continue praying for him, since God had decided to end his regime and clear the country of his soldiers. He told me to go to a particular place in Kabowa village two miles away and sit on a stone that I would find in a certain old man's compound. I found out later the man's name was Musisi. The angel told me that a woman dressed in white would come out of the house and ask me why I was sitting on the stone. Also he said that a white car with the number plate UVS 888 would park in the compound at the same time. The angel added that when I saw the car I would know that I had found the right place. Another white car would come and park in the compound and this car would give me a lift back home later. I should not be afraid if all these people were to crouch over me to interview me. Soon a large group of people gathered round me joining Musisi and his wife so I was standing in the middle of about sixty people. They were all born-again Christians meeting secretly in a garage since the ban on their churches.

As I told them my story I could see them beginning to trust me. When I mentioned the white car with the registration UVS 888 they all recognised it was a car belonging to one of their members. It arrived very soon after this and so they came to trust me more and more. It parked very near to where I was standing and speaking to them. They all shouted, 'Glory to God!' The old lady dressed in the traditional white Kiganda robe said, 'I thought at the beginning you were an Amin's spy but I thank God you are not.' Mr. Musisi, her husband, asked 'When will Amin fall?'

The angel had given me the date, exactly five months from that date.

'Raise your right hands,' I said, 'count loudly one by one, the fingers of that hand.' They very happily did so.

'One ... two ... three ... four ... Five!'

'In exactly five months – sometime in the middle of April next year. When it happens, you will remember what I told you.'

After this, many members of that group would come to look for me at the school I was now working in. I had left the Anglican school and was now working for a Muslim head. They would ask me to pray for them and we would see many answers to our prayers. So many miracles happened that the headmaster was really perplexed by what he called my 'new thing'. He asked me to choose between the new thing and my job! I chose my new thing, of course. Having been dismissed from another school, I decided I had better earn my living by painting. Art was not very popular as very few people could afford it, so to make the most money I specialised in painting portraits that were irresistible to those who did have the money.

I dreamed one night that an angel showed me a house that I was later to rent. It was an older, abandoned building with no doors or windows. It was flanked by tall trees and overgrown bushes and inhabited by rats, snakes, cockroaches and lizards. I found the house and its owner who agreed to let me live in the property rent-free. He believed the house was haunted by evil spirits and didn't think I would live there for very long. It was also a well-known dumping ground for stolen property and a notorious hideout for thieves and robbers. Many of the people I met at Kabowa came to see me at home to ask for private prayer. When the numbers visiting us continued to rise, I decided to buy the house. It is now the site of the Namirembe Christian Fellowship.

Early in the morning of April 11th, anti-Amin fighters reached Kampala. April 11th 1979 said the calendar on my wall. Idi Amin's regime was overthrown amid deafening cries of joy! What a relief! But it was a little soon for rejoicing. The governments that followed were little better than the old for several more years. For seven years the culture of murder continued after Amin's departure. However, those who had been present when I had prophesied the date of Amin's fall went around preaching vigorously that Jesus is alive. Yes, Amin may have killed the archbishop, but on April 11th God proved He was greater than Amin. I regard my fearlessness today as being directly related to that incident. The group I had spoken to at the Kabowa stone were greatly encouraged in their faith as a result of the miracle. If they had not seen for themselves the miracle of Amin's fall as I had prophesied earlier, they would not have believed it. A huge church has now been erected near the place where I sat on the stone. It is called Kabowa Redeemed church. The stone I sat on has been preserved to keep the memory alive. They will never forget the first day they saw me. Pastor Elijah invites me each year on the anniversary to preach; no longer am I Amin's spy, now I am an honourable guest at their 'old boy' conferences.

Chapter 3

Defeating Witchcraft

I like to call the miracles I have witnessed the works of God's hand. The word 'hand' in the Bible, when talking about the works of God's hand, refers particularly to God's strength and power expressed in a physical act. In Hebrew the word translated most often in the phrase 'the hand of the Lord' is the word transliterated as *yad*. The phrase 'the hand of the Lord' expresses deliverance and freedom as a result of God moving in real power to change our circumstances or our perception. God is working to free you from the authority you have previously been subjected to, which makes a distinct difference that you can feel. You can perceive by physical, psychological and spiritual means God moving invisibly. When God's hand is at work, you can know that God is backing up your declaration with His power to make a tangible difference. When you act in obedience to His leading, He follows through for His people. Christianity is not just a verbal presentation of the oracles of God; it is also a call to demonstrate God's nature triumphing over the forces of darkness.

The world in which we live today once existed as a mere project in the mind of God. There was then a shift from the level where we were just a bright idea in His mind to a new value called 'people, the earth and all that is in it'. If God had not turned His thoughts into value, we would not exist. This is my idea about biblical promises. If there is no way in our heart that we can turn God's promises into their physical equivalent, we will never see miracles. This is true with all knowledge. Knowledge not turned into value is worthless. Jesus has taught us that if we truly believe we will perform miracles. That means we will subdue diseases, political systems, and all forces of darkness. A system in which violation of rules, destruction of good and decay are allowed to go unchecked ends up in extinction. That is why Jesus is Saviour. Salvation is in place to keep our race from extinction.

In addition to God's sovereign acts of power believers have power to perform miracles. The Bible teaches that we believers have been delegated authority to crush the kingdom of Satan wherever we go. We are actually placed into God's supernatural strategy, not based on common sense, but in His power to set captives free. That's what I understood when Jesus met me and told me to wake up and read Isaiah chapter 60.

> *'Arise and shine;*
> *For your light has come!*
> *And the **glory of the** Lord **is** risen upon you.*
> *For behold, the darkness shall cover the earth.*
> *And deep darkness the people;*
> *But the* Lord *will arise over you.*
> *And **His glory** will be seen upon you.'*   (Isaiah 60:1–2)

These scriptures, of course, have a different historical and theological meaning for the Jewish people, but Jesus meant these words to define my destiny as well. God intended not only Amin's defeat by these words, but He intends you and me to defeat witchdoctors as well.

Rachel Nnampija had an amazing deliverance from danger in the early days of our ministry. She now works as a care assistant at St Ebbes Hospital in London. I met her again on October 29th 2000 in the Agape Miracle Centre Church at Deptford, Lewisham Way, UK. She was all smiles, delighted her testimony will be published, calling herself a 'valuable antique' as we remembered the incident which happened 19 years ago when she was a member of Namirembe Christian Fellowship. In 1981 many people would turn up at my house without warning, trying to escape from being killed or maimed by pursuing soldiers who would often do house to house searches without warning during the night. Even after Idi Amin's fall, this practice went on for some years and some 800,000 Ugandan people were killed or injured this way.

One evening over thirty people came to seek refuge in our home. Among them was Rachel. We huddled together and prayed. We prayed for each other for specific issues and for the awful gloom that hung over our country. Our prayer time was especially deep and passionate that night as we poured out our pain and faith, and many times we spoke in tongues and saw visions. Judas Tadaeus was healed at that same meeting. His body had become all twisted up because of an illness he had had for 29 years. We were all overjoyed when I gave him a command in Jesus' name and he stretched out his legs and arms, and stood on his feet for the first time. Not only did he walk, he jumped and he danced as well. At the end of the meeting, just before people got ready to sleep, I warned people to beware of a poisonous snake because I had seen a vision of a witchdoctor sending a snake to bite and kill someone called Rachel Nnampija.

Rachel had left her safari bed in one of the rooms. She picked it up to check and that was when I heard loud screams from the other girls who were with her. Right under her bed was an angry cobra. It was weaving backwards and forwards, just about to strike, its fangs huge in the stiffened open mouth. Everybody rushed into the room. 'Where is it?' we all exclaimed to each other in awe because of the word I had not long spoken. We struck him dead. Rachel had miraculously escaped danger and she lives to tell the tale to this day.

God still speaks today to His people through the super-natural gift of prophecy. A person who has cleverly reasoned out a message, or arrived at his 'word' after some private calculation or skill, is not likely to be communicating a direct prophecy from God. You may have attended meetings where you have seen people interrupt the proceedings, sometimes quite disruptively, blurting out their message without any self-control at all. Such an immature act is not good. It calls God's reputation into question. God is orderly and when He puts a message in someone's heart it is a deep-felt calling, perceived strongly within, but at the same time able to be communicated modestly and with politeness. It is an assignment from God, which the person has no doubt comes from Him. It is too real, beautiful and honest; a sight far beyond your own imagination, too beyond the human eye, that you know only too well within you it is God who has done it. Even though I have described it, there is still more to discover about this gift, for it is through God's action that you know it is God's message, that it is indeed God who is speaking, that you discern God's voice. Our human mechanisms of perception and communication are too limited also so that no-one has the perfect ability to discern correctly all the time.

Often people will say things they think are from God, but actually they are just coming from their own desire to help and comfort. Even worse, some contributions may be concoctions which originate from inner pride and a desire to be noticed. Others simply tell deliberate lies. The Bible teaches us that we should not meekly take every utterance at face value when the speaker declares he has a word from God. Rather we should evaluate each prophecy in the light of God's Word. This process we call exercising spiritual discernment. Many mistakes happen in this area in Charismatic and Pentecostal churches. The leaders of these congregations, in particular, should be careful, for they risk the spectacle of honest crowds witnessing the Lord's Spirit being publicly held up to ridicule. In some places I have even heard well-rehearsed messages calculated to embarrass their husband, wife, friend, enemy

etc. At Namirembe Christian Fellowship we call such utter-
ances 'a convenient whip'. Imagine how the pastor feels in
this situation! I tell you, the Holy Spirit is extremely grieved by
the use of such a whip in His Name! The lone, non-church
attending private prophet or prophetess can commit even
worse offences. You should look before you leap if you want to
be safe. Not all that glitters is gold.

There are many motives for the misuse of the gift of
prophecy we see in our churches. Many people are looking
for opportunities to get attention. They want to be looked up
to as someone special. Others, quite frankly, are out for
financial gain. Or they are simply confused. Whatever their
motive, the end is the same. They are all out to target you and
your soul. By the time you realise they made a mistake they
have messed up a quarter of your lifetime. So, be careful, do
not always listen undiscriminatingly!

God's words of prophecy are communicated with His attitude of graciousness, mercy and love to our hearts. The warmth
of His heart accompanies the message. The apostle Paul says
we should not stop fellowshipping with our brethren. Famil-
iarity with God's Word helps us to know what actually His will
is. His will, what pleases Him, is clearly written in Scripture. We
should study God's Word carefully, like one would study the
works of art of a great painter such as Van Gogh, or Picasso. By
this means we come to recognise the style and characteristics
of the artist. In the same way when we study God's Word
we come to recognise the characteristic style of the author. We
will quickly be able to distinguish the origin of a particular
message, whether God or Satan. Likewise we can differentiate a
real miracle from a satanic supernatural counterfeit.

Judging wickedness

In New Testament days there were instances where God
punished directly and decisively those who deliberately

displayed disobedience. In Acts 5 the Holy Spirit punished Ananias and Sapphira with death. This was caused by God, not Peter. We should not attribute God's work to either Satan or to the prophet. It would be blasphemy to call God's work the work of either a man or the devil. Their death was a holy explosion of spiritual power unleashed to teach obedience in a way that would reverberate through the hearts of people, both then and now, so we all would fear God. Taking God for granted can spoil us and leave our churches open to evil infiltration, whereas the Church should be holy. God is a real person. He has real feelings. He has a heart. God is the same yesterday, today and tomorrow. He is also judge, a judge yesterday, today and tomorrow. His judgement is always right.

Sayuni's healing

One day in 1983, Sayuni Kaserebe Adyeri of Bugungu-Hoima District in Uganda was carried on a stretcher into the evening service in a coma, as I was preaching. It was in those gloomy days of political turmoil, and the hospitals had a difficult time. Due to major inefficiency, many people died because of neglect or inappropriate medical attention. As a result, many resorted to witchdoctors. One such was Sayuni, who was at the point of death when she was brought to the service. She had come two hundred miles in this critical condition. When Sayuni was first taken ill, she was well enough for the witch-doctor to add her to his large number of 'wives'. Soon Sayuni could stand the guilt no more and rejected his advances vigorously. This made the man very angry. When she left the compound without his permission, he flew into a rage and sent a curse after her. At once she became much more ill and declined into a coma. Just before she lost consciousness completely, someone reminded her of the miracles that were happening in Namirembe Christian Fellowship. In fact she had visited once out of curiosity, before she got sick, and had seen a deaf boy healed. This gave her hope that Jesus might heal her too.

As she was placed in front of me, the Holy Spirit prompted me to prophesy that however sick she appeared, she would be used as a gospel instrument to impact her home district strongly after she was healed.

The situation looked hopeless. To all outward appearances, prayer was a complete waste of time. Some of the men who accompanied her said they had better be starting home with her since she was so far gone. Several of her relatives looked at me and burst into tears. I really can't think why. Teary eyes were not the way to face this situation. This was no time for tears, this was time for action. I had to raise their faith by asking them to see the situation not in their own way, but through the eyes of God and focus on the miracle He could do for her, irrespective of the many signals to the contrary. The battle was not ours, but the Lord's. God made man out of dust. The whole human race originated out of dust, insignificant, nothing dust. With God nothing is impossible (Luke 1:37).

Sayuni's skin looked yellow and wrinkled, like a dried tobacco leaf. She was severely dehydrated, huge cracks at the corners of her mouth, hopelessly in extremis. She appeared to be only a moment or two away from breathing her last. She was just a tiny, anaemic, framework of a miserably perishing woman. A proper picture of death. Her mouth sagging open, she obviously needed total nursing care. Numbed by months of pain, with clenched fists and anxious expression she would confusedly murmur disjointed syllables. Her nurse would try and calm her, 'Jesus loves you, Sayuni'.

I noticed immediately the usual cajolery exercised by loved ones around the very ill, when you say all the sweet, soothing things you can while their life slowly ebbs away. The children crowded round her, making her attendant cross. From time to time a tear would trickle down her cheek. Older women started to cry in sympathy, probably remembering their own relatives' demises. Sayuni's slowly dying body lay in front of us all. Perhaps the earthen altar would not wait to take its sacrifice until the end of the service, when we would usually pray for the sick. I shouted, 'That you may know that Jesus lives today, let that lady be healed so she may attend to those souls in the revival about to break out in her home area!' From that moment Sayuni began to recover. Immediately I saw a change in her eyes. In two hours she had regained normal consciousness. In fact she does not remember getting to the service, but she remembers leaving. Her appetite and strength improved steadily and by the end of one month she was completely well.

Root cause, the witchdoctor's curse

Nebaoth Rubyamengo was the powerful witchdoctor responsible for the curse that had been killing Sayuni. Seated on his little wooden stool, smoking a huge curse pipe, Nebaoth would brag that he was king of the witchdoctors whose reign would never end.

Now she was healed, Sayuni was determined to resist any more predatory passes made at her by this crafty strongman. In her bag she now carried a Bible and was prepared to use the power Jesus delegates to believers. She knew Nebaoth would be unable to stand against her as long as God stood by her side. God's promises, which she had heard repeated in our preaching, resounded in her head like African victory drums:

> *'Whoever assembles against you shall fall for your sake ...*
> *No weapon formed against you shall prosper.*
> *And every tongue which rises against you in judgment*
> *You shall condemn.'* (Isaiah 54:15–17)

She believed this. But six months later she came to see me, shaking like a leaf, a quivering, emotional jelly. Nebaoth had sent a message to her via a fully qualified nurse. He said he was going to kill both me and her in seven days time. Well, Sayuni just caved in. Her self-esteem collapsed. She was far too weak to trust God. I told Sayuni to be strong. Nebaoth had said 'seven days and we would be dead', unless we apologised to him. How come a witchdoctor can be so confident of his power in the devil and yet we be so weak in God? NO way, honey!

One of the main problems I faced when God called me to this ministry was the reaction of religious people. They did not seem to be concerned when God's name was being put down. Prophets and apostles in the Bible would never have been so tolerant. They would not have allowed such remarks to go unchallenged. What is wrong with our modern-day prophets? How dare a witchdoctor ever think of threatening to kill us? No way! God reigns all mighty, for ever.

I said to Sayuni, 'No! Nebaoth had better turn to God within seven days.' If we died within seven days, he had better watch out on the eighth. God would be sure to defend His Name on the eighth day. So we prayed and I sent her home. She returned, full of joy, her fist raised high, screaming 'Mukama Asiimwe, Praise the Lord!' It was reported to us that Nebaoth had not repented and died on the eighth day.

On the eighth day, as promised when he didn't get his apology, Nebaoth tried to call down a curse on both of us. Unfortunately for him, instead of harming us, it rebounded on his own house. A fire burned his house, in fact a ball of fire just dropped out of the sky. The articles used in magical arts that he kept under his bed and the man himself were consumed by the fire. His wife and children were unharmed; but oddly, the bed under which he had stored all the tools of his trade was not burned. News of this miracle hit the headlines and many thousands of Western Ugandans repented and turned to Jesus as a result.

A study of witchcraft

In 1994 an American friend and I paid a visit to the Kasubi Royal Tombs. This is a well-known centre of witchcraft and we were going to get a first-hand account of some of these evil practices. This place is the burial ground of the Buganda kings and is visited by many to seek the witchdoctor's assistance in gaining power over people they would like to influence, for example people they would like to have sex with, or family members they would like to see harmed out of spite.

The tomb's librarian directed us to a huge mud and wattle hut nearby, owned by an elderly woman. We had to pay her for our consultation. Inside the building was a raised platform where she would go to sit and invoke the spirits. The proceedings began with her musicians prostrating themselves before her and playing a fast, lively song accompanied by much skilled drumming and clapping. A fourteen-year-old virgin danced in a frenzy. Manifestly excited, the priestess lit her pipe and started conversing with demonic spirits as if she was speaking to birds hovering in front of her. At the end of all this fuss she told us:

'I received this power from grandfather's spirits. They travel all over the world doing god's work and are called different names by the different tribes of the world. There are so many gods who were declared null and void when Christianity began to be practised, but they exist and have been doing their work on earth. Some of these are royal spirits, which can do anything, using both humans and beasts. They are so powerful that this white lady who came with you, if ordered to do what she does not want to, including removing all her clothes and running naked, will be compelled to do so until they are appeased.

'We use these spirits to punish, protect and bless. These spears, fetishes, pipes, drums, musical instruments and even much more, which we will not show you, can be used either as objects of appeasement or punishment. When patients come here, we sometimes make light cuts into their skin and fix fetishes into their bodies. Sometimes we require them to come with a calabash of beer, or a chicken or goat to talk to their ancestors, depending on what they are asking for. They then take back the head of the slaughtered goat or chicken and some medicine and do according to their heart's desire. Sometimes they take back some of the blood and sprinkle it where thy want to. The grandfathers will then sniff around the sites where the blood has been sprinkled and then they know what to do.

'If anyone is pejorative of the power we use, we can then open "mortar" fire (send a curse) at him. The grandfathers (demons) will caress these objects and recall what was done by dead warriors using the same objects and get emboldened to attack anyone most fiercely. It would then occur to him that he did wrong. We have power here, we can do everything or anything, mention what you like.' They all burst into laughter at our ignorance.

'For example,' she continued, 'this spear and that sword belong to a great warrior king of the past. If we want to deal with some stubborn people who by becoming Christians have refused to honour us and the spirits of our ancestors, we can use them to scratch his skin a little, swear by the deceased king's name and send him to weaken them. People we send this way can pay a short visit to the targeted person or to the church where he prays and that's it. This is how many religious leaders come here as well. We are Christians too. We combine both.'

A large number of people, including self-professed Christians, have come to see me privately in every country I have visited, confessing to having had involvement with witch-doctors. Some have swallowed fetishes, or been scratched by a witchdoctor's knife, or have had creams or herbs inserted into their body or blood stream. Some have been required to supply things for the witchdoctor, especially pubic hair, underwear, or small pieces taken from the clothes of their enemies. I have heard of people who have surreptitiously fed their spouses faeces or urine. Bizarrely, some have eaten their own faeces or drunk cat's urine, in order to appease the gods.

Some more extreme requirements include having sex with the witchdoctor, or the murder of children, babies or women in exchange for some kind of luck. I sometimes wonder if this might contribute to the motivation behind some apparently motiveless murders. It was said that Idi Amin was asked to kill his own son and eat his heart. Even highly respected professionals such as doctors or nurses have been known to visit witchdoctors or psychics. One of my own choir members once told me her mother used to pick up dust from her footprints and put it in plastic bags. It would end up at a witchdoctor's. The witchdoctor would have demons invoked with a view to controlling this choir member's life. The choir member's mother was especially angry because of her uncompromising faith in God.

Witchdoctors expect their followers to remain loyal to them, so we have a war to fight and a devil to deliver people from. Right at this moment Satan is travelling back and forth on the earth trying to squash everything good which God is doing in order to blind as many people as possible and woo worshippers to himself. The Bible says *'And the* LORD *said to Satan, "From where do you come?" So Satan answered the* LORD *and said "From going to and fro on the earth, and from walking back and forth on it . . . "'* (Job 1:7).

The word 'Sa-hatan' is the Hebrew from which we get the name Satan. Satan is not a proper name but a description. His true name is Lucifer, but he is given different names in each country, all descriptive names of Lucifer and his demons. 'Sa-hatan' means 'hateful enemy'. The devil is a hater of both God and man. If we read the book of Job, we see that he works very hard and covers a lot of space on earth in a very short time. God asked, *'From where do you come?'* Satan answered, *'From going to and fro on the earth and from walking back and forth on it.'* Satan goes back and forth on earth doing things he is not authorised to do. The church was sent for this reason, to destroy the works of the devil, because they were not authorised by God. Jesus said that Lazarus' sickness was not meant to end in death at that time. Yet Lazarus died. So Jesus woke him up. What should be our response if Lazarus had not come back to life? How should we react if the miracle does not happen?

We should not lose our faith just because a miracle does not happen. One day death will be defeated. Everything that holds out now will be unable to do so on the last day. If you lose your faith because someone dies, you will sure be unhappy when they are resurrected when death is finally defeated! It is public knowledge that death was defeated when Jesus was resurrected. So death keeps its victims only for a short period of time.

If I were in God's panel of judges, I would ask Satan, 'Walking back and forth on earth doing what? What business have you got to do with the earth?' Jesus teaches that Satan is a liar from the beginning, and he is the father of all lies. 'You are of your father, the devil and the desires of your father you want to do,' I say to all demons. 'The devil was a murderer from the very beginning and does not stand in the truth, because there is no truth in him. When he speaks a lie, he speaks from his own resources for he is a liar and the father of all lies.'

The reason God puts a hedge around us, like he did for Job, is because He is aware that there is this invisible, negative power full of hatred, who is very busy raiding us. He goes back and forth on the earth accusing, resisting, obstructing, hindering, destroying and killing whatever is good.

> *'Does Job fear God for nothing? Have You not made a hedge around him, around his household, and around all that he has*

> *on every side? You have blessed the work of his hands, and his*
> *possessions have increased in the land.'* (Job 1:9–10)

Satan was so jealous that he asked God to abandon the man, Job, who He had created. He also asked God to let him harm Job, accusing Job of only serving God for gain, not out of genuine love and faith towards God. So God allowed Satan to test Job.

> *'"Behold, all that he has is in your power; only do not lay a*
> *hand on his person." So Satan went out from the presence of*
> *the LORD.'* (Job 1:12)

In other words he went back to his occupation of walking back and forth on earth to do more of his hateful work. Job was found unyieldingly faithful, in spite of being cruelly tested by Satan.

> *'Naked I came from my mother's womb,*
> *And naked shall I return there.*
> *The LORD gave, and the LORD has taken away;*
> *Blessed be the name of the LORD.'* (Job 1:21)

Faithfulness is very important. In Daniel's case it was because of his faithfulness to God that his associates made negative reports against him and had him thrown into the lion's den. We may also have to suffer for being faithful to God. Because of his faithfulness Daniel was saved from being eaten by the lions. The lions mysteriously lost their appetites and did not tear him to pieces. Job too was vindicated for his faith, and after God allowed his time of suffering, He blessed his latter days more than his beginning. God had permitted Satan's attack on Job to show that even in the face of adversity, Job would not turn away from Him.

Jesus, who said that Satan steals, kills and destroys, happily

gave believers the power to trample on serpents and scor-
pions and over all the power of the enemy. Satan hates the
protection that we have been given by God in the name of
Jesus. Today human beings inhabit the entire surface of the
earth. At one time Satan had only Adam and Eve to visit. Now
he is very busy visiting so many. He prefers that many stay
unborn, and others remain blind to the fact that believers
have been given the power to drive him out, as Mark 16:17
declares.

Though spectacular, involvement with witchdoctors and
psychics as illustrated by such examples as Sayuni's story, are
easy to avoid as they are obviously evil. Less detectable as evil
were the kind of beliefs I held before I met Jesus, which were
also inspired by Satan. Most people would have attributed my
beliefs to my own human nature. Atheism, humanism and
vanity would appear acceptable, and would certainly seem
intellectually to have no connection whatsoever with Satan.
Television programmes portraying increasing debauchery,
witchcraft, occult practices and violence flood national chan-
nels but are accepted as normal behaviour.

Satan has another side to his nature. He is also the tempter.
We have all known temptation. The tempter is not immediately apparent as the cause of the temptation because he
works indirectly. If there are consequences to falling for
temptation, we would usually take all the blame and face the
music alone. The tempter is also a liar. The world today is all
twisted up by the deceit of an invisible evil called Lucifer.
There is widespread acceptance of practices that used to be
taboo, and an increasing tendency to ridicule Christianity as
outdated by using examples of abuse of trust to prove God's
lack of power. Not everyone respects witchdoctors and
psychics, but many are proud to declare themselves atheist
or gay, openly seeking to gain acceptance for their lifestyle by
media campaigns. Public opinion, fuelled by the media, has
the power to change government policy. It is not an accident

that the media lends itself to influence from these ungodly appeals. Ours is a very relaxed society, where all wrongs are attributed to ignorance which can be righted by the activity of politicians, scientists, lawyers and society. My own opinion is that this insidious slide of moral standards is due to the devious influence of Satan behind the scenes, who is continuing his work of prowling back and forth in the world just as he did in Eve's day. His aim is to OK rebellion against God in every corner of the earth. David says in Psalm 14:

> 'The fool has said in his heart,
> "There is no God."'   (Psalm 14:1)

King David had seen so many miracles during his life that to mention the possibility that God does not exist was not just ignorant, it was downright foolish. Before we prove that God exists by signs and wonders, we should be prepared to be called fools, but after we have proved that God exists and still people won't believe, we might be excused for joining David and calling the rest of the world foolish.

This book is about miracles. I have seen miracles. I have evidence to prove to the world that God exists. I am prepared to testify in a court of law, in English, French or Luganda the nature of my evidence to prove my claim. I am prepared to speak in any medical school, university or parliament to justify this declaration. I know that God will support me with even more miracles to vindicate my claim before any doubting forum. Things that should not have happened, happened to me since Jesus came into my life.

In Acts 1:8 the promise of this power is directly linked to our calling to be Jesus' witnesses. The promise is directly tied down to our responsibility to witness. A witness in a court of law is someone who sees an event take place and is subsequently asked to describe it to others. In court one gives evidence after swearing to tell the truth. Sworn evidence must not be vague. The trial must prove beyond reasonable doubt that the defendant has done the action of which he is accused.

We are called to heal all manner of diseases as evidence to prove beyond reasonable doubt that Jesus is alive. This should include healing victims of accidents, using God's power to heal their fractured bones, torn muscles and ligaments, impaired nerves and damaged brains. It should include healing people with AIDS, cancer, leprosy, and all manner of complications. It should also include raising people from the dead. These miracles are in order to answer the crucial question, about which we are obliged to tell the truth. The Bible describes the Lord Jesus, through the prophets, the apostles and the gospel accounts as Lord of lords, King of kings and as possessing all authority in heaven and on earth. This claim must be proved here on earth without any possibility of reasonable doubt. This is why Jesus told me 'I will be with you wherever you go to perform miracles and wonders by which people will know that I have sent you.'

It must be remembered that in order for Jesus to make these promises, He must first defeat death. When Jesus appeared after the resurrection He did not have weeping wounds. He was pierced through His flesh in a number of places when He endured the process of murder by crucifixion. When He was finally believed to be dead, the Roman soldier had to prove this by thrusting a spear into His side; this was a recognised technical procedure that was often applied to test for death of crucifixion victims. If the victim was dead, both water and blood would pour out of the wound. If still alive, it would finally put the victim out of his misery, since this technical procedure results in the spear tip ending in the heart.

The Bible records the flow of water mixed with blood, which splashed out of Jesus' body. So having certified death, He was placed in a tomb. Even after death, Jesus was still a political threat, so guards were deployed outside the tomb.

Jesus' resurrection miracle was so feared by the government that they even kept Him a prisoner when dead. The resurrection of Jesus shows that His power, power bequeathed to us, can go against all the odds. The soldiers were defeated. His wounds were healed, His blood, water and life restored. Lacerated muscles, damaged nerves and ligaments, perforated heart, all were dealt with by the power of God. Restored by the very power we have been promised!

Jesus' body was a human, natural body just the same as ours is, a human body made for Him by God as our bodies are also.

> 'Therefore, when He came into the world, He said:
> "Sacrifice and offering You did not desire
> But a body you have prepared for Me."'   (Hebrews 10:5)

The power of God can heal all physical bruises. By receiving this same power we are authorised by God to deal with this area too. The resurrection of Jesus was a great miracle. Believers have therefore a heavy calling. We have a lot to prove. We have a big testimony to prove which is humanly speaking inconceivable. It needs God.

Jesus' body did not rot, unlike that of Lazarus who was also raised from death. As we read in John 11:39 Martha says, 'By now it will give off a bad smell.' It means that the death of Lazarus was a conclusive fact. The spear in his ribs proved Jesus' death. Every organ of Lazarus' body was dead. Living was a forgotten idea for Lazarus. The body was decomposing; you can't get a more desperate situation than that. Yet at Bethany, the object of the wake was resurrected! By the power of Jesus, which we are to receive when we believe, Lazarus was restored to being a normal living man. Many Jews from all religious persuasions came especially to see him. Religious men were so offended that they plotted to kill him a second time. Tradition says he fled to Cyprus where he founded a church which still exists in spite of years spent under Moslem control.

Someone is annoyed by Jesus' power.

The power we receive challenges and annoys our opponent. It proves our case beyond reasonable doubt, so it may provoke him to anger. The case we are giving our evidence for is this, the proof of Jesus' Lordship in heaven and earth. Our evidence leaves Satan intellectually and factually empty handed before the bench of the world court. Jesus told His disciples to turn people of all nations into His witnesses, His disciples (Matthew 28:18–20).

The job to which Jesus' disciples are called and for which they are to receive God's power is to *'cast out unclean spirits, heal all manner of sicknesses, and all kinds of disease, to preach that the kingdom of heaven is at hand, to cleanse the lepers, raise the dead'* (see Matthew 10:1 & 8). To be good at this job we have to develop a strong attitude against the devil and negative forces of nature. We have to be new creatures. Nothing should overwhelm us if we are to be effective disciples. Above all, we must be wise in our discipleship.

> *'Behold, I send you out as sheep in the midst of wolves. Therefore be wise as serpents and harmless as doves.'*
> (Matthew 10:16)

We have also to be aware of an important fact. People are likely to be opposed to us because of our faith in Jesus and the things we are likely to do because of it. Some of the amazing things we do may arouse jealousy or hatred in others that can increase to the point where even our relatives or other preachers join in plotting our destruction. Jesus said we would be hated *'by all for My name's sake.'* This might seem unbearable to us but we can be reassured that *'he who endures to the end will be saved'* (Matthew 10:22), but read also the context in the preceding verses, 10:17–21. Remember Daniel? Because he was faithful to God, Daniel's enemies, also incidentally not loyal to King Darius, tricked the king into throwing him into the lion's den. Because of his same faithfulness, God rescued Daniel from being eaten. Jesus told His disciples they would be true disciples only if they were ready to carry their cross.

In the book of Revelation we see the Lord promising to reward overcomers. We have a glimpse of the parallel worlds of heaven and earth. In the heavenly setting, there is God with His angels ready to fight, on the earth an adversary called Satan, who pursues disciples with persecution, and continually contests faith in God. To our minds faith is a comfort, but to the mind of God it is war. Paul tells us to be strong in Ephesians 6:10, and to put on the whole armour, armour designed to protect when on the offensive, with little protection for the back. Jesus says that we should be brave. We have to achieve victory. He has defeated the world. So let us rise to the occasion. It's war. There are prizes to be won. You cannot just sit back and watch everything good your God has given be destroyed by men under Satan's influence. You must go out into battle.

Chapter 4

A Vision of Hell and Heaven

I used to be offended at some of the things I read in the Bible. Frankly they seemed to be false, invented tall stories. But as time has passed I have become sure that the entire Bible is real and factual. We know, for example, that Jesus Christ was a real person; also He is a real person who exists today. I know that this real person has supernatural power. I also know that the devil exists too, and he operates through such means as witchcraft, palmistry, astrology, the worship of dead ancestors, or even the worship of people who were faithful believers in their lifetime, or fake images.

Does the hereafter really exist?

Celia and I had been married for about four years when an awesome thing happened one night around midnight, just before I fell asleep. A strange light filtered through the roof of our bedroom and settled over me like a shining sheet. At the same time I felt myself being taken upwards. Beside me was an angel who helped me understand that I was going to heaven. I do not know how long the journey took us, I lost all sense of time, but at last I found I was standing on the edge of a cliff, overlooking hell. I felt extremely far away from the earth. We were somewhere far away from the known universe. It was so remote we seemed to have crossed many time zones. Here on earth, if you take a plane, the captain will tell you from time to

55

time the local time at the place you are travelling over. When on a long-haul flight local time ceases to have any meaning after a while. Now try to imagine you are travelling across the universe, the same thing happening on a much grander scale. Your sense of time diminishes until it vanishes. You have crossed so many time zones and solar systems that the whole idea of time and life on earth seems insignificant, almost meaningless, a void. It is like trying to identify with a relative who died four thousand years ago. Where time no longer exists you are in a new culture, the realm of eternity. All things have meaning and make sense only because they exist in God. This is how I am attempting to explain how this journey felt. The earth seemed a distant, past shadow. All earthly attractions had vanished from my heart. I stood at a watershed where power, status, human dignity and ambition disappear into insignificant obscurity. I felt ashamed of my earthly ambitions as totally out of place here. Whenever I remember that night, you better believe me, I am chilled to the bone because I realise that millions of people are going to face this same point later who are now engaged in all sorts of evil activities! There will come a time for every person when they will come face to face with God Himself.

Belt of fire

Over the cliff I saw a huge valley filled with fire. It was divided into three blazing worlds of torture. Imagine New York, Moscow or London as the Sahara Desert full of people writhing in agony. The place was so hot it seemed God had ordered any cooling wind to depart from the vicinity, so that the atmosphere itself was on fire. The valley was a prison for those who had committed offences against heaven. I call it the belt of fire. It seemed to me that there was a boundary, like the customs boundary of a country, so that nobody could get in without going through a screening procedure first. The people had real bodies; they were real persons, not just moving shadows. There were three distinct levels of torture in the belt of fire, three worlds into which bodies were diving, diving into a pit of multiple tortures. It was as if when people die, they just walk back into the body they had before they were born. That's what I thought, because the body I was in felt real. I felt no different. This body is immortal. It is not just a state of mind; the body has bones, flesh, and a type of human frailty when compared to the bodies of angels. Angels have bodies too, they are physical, but they are also able to travel beyond the speed of electrons.

Matter is simply the constant movement of electrons around the nucleus at a certain speed. If you were able to travel faster than this speed you would be able to defy the hindrance of things in the way of your passing. The friction set up as you passed through the obstacles would cause heat to be generated; in effect you would be creating fire. I do not fully understand how heavenly power operates. Heaven does not operate with the same set of physical laws that govern our universe. When I notice new things about the ways of heaven I like to try and understand how they work. Science may well find it impossible to investigate because there is such a difference in the world as we know it and the science of creation hidden in the mind of God. God has His secrets that He has not yet revealed to us.

Crossing the valley

Earth seemed very distant. An authoritative voice gave us just one short minute to decide whether to attempt to fly over the valley of fire to heaven beyond. I watched many others taking that decision to begin their flight. Some made it all the way, others, having failed to cross to the other bank, sank to their predetermined level in the horrible fire. I understood in that moment that earth is where people make the decision which determines whether you get to heaven or hell. I saw many people in this vision face the sorting process; some were cleared for heaven, and the rest belonged to hell. Hell was intelligent. The fire selected those who were to remain and those to let go. If anyone had harboured a grudge, he especially was dragged down by the weight of his heart that had turned into a heavy metal ball, like the shot used by athletes in a shot-put competition. I saw several people slide down into the inferno.

I was not there on the edge of the cliff observing for very long; just enough time to see three kinds of fire and to comprehend the three denoted levels of sin and the commensurate punishment. The uppermost one, on top, was amber in colour, the middle one was so hot it was like the blue flame of a Bunsen burner and at the bottom was a black flame mixed with a miasma of offensive smoke and ugly tar. The place was agony in its totality. It was a place where 'wise' sinners could stay foolish forever. It was a place where those who had died faithful would shine out brightly to be envied, a place of regret for the deceived of the earth to feel eternal remorse.

My turn

My angel, the one who had brought me to this place, had changed his clothes and now wore what looked to me like a bridal garment. I saw him fly across the abyss. When he was half way over his example gave me confidence to follow. My identity was in Christ, not in hell. Those who identified with the perishable attractions of the world perished with their prize, their reward, in the belt of torture. Those who have their heart hidden in the Rock of Ages abide in Him. I had no fear of falling into the pit, due to the love I have for Him. The warmth of the fire helped me to float across. What an irony that the fire, a curse to some, was to those who love the Lord a blessing. It was kind in that it, too, served the interest of God's people rather than the devil's. In hell, Satan is not master, God is! Satan is a victim too. He too is a prisoner.

The angel waited for me until I landed. He was very tall and in order to listen to the short man he was talking to, walked with a stoop. He was to guide me to where Jesus was and to familiarise me with heaven. To be here felt great.

Walking in heaven

Heaven looks like a most beautiful, massive version of earth. I really can say it is paradise. There is grass, trees, footpaths and an atmosphere. But you can't compare its beauty to anything we know on earth. Everything in heaven is alive and intelligent. For example I saw a river flowing in two streams, side by side, of milk and water which did not mix. It knew whether a person had the right to drink of it or not. As we walked towards the river, I was allowed to look more closely at Earth, which in comparison looked a 90% dead mass. Everything on Earth looked so worthless, like a cheap replica.

I realised that my own parents were like hired baby-sitters. When we meet in heaven it will be very clear to our mother and father that they are not the true parents, as they had always believed. The Lord God Himself, our Creator, is our true parent. Matthew 23:9 says,

> *'Do not call anyone on earth your father; for One is your Father, He who is in heaven.'*

Therefore it makes no sense at all to try and put Mary, Jesus' earthly mother, in the exalted position of mother of God. The very moment you mention God, you are talking about heavenly matters where things are completely different. But even if you stick to the time when Mary lived on earth, no-one ever worshipped her at that time. No-one prayed to her, or via her. This appalling twist of faith should be avoided. The Bible does not teach that Mary was the mother of God. We had better be sticking to the mind of God as revealed in His Word. There is no comparison between your Creator and mere man who was only ordered by God to produce and multiply the human race on the surface of earth. Adam had only one father, who was God; he had no-one else as father because he was the first. Jesus, the 'second Adam' also had no earthly father.

It is good that He had no earthly father. If He had He would have been plagued by the genetic inheritance of their sinful acts. So, He would not have been quite as strong as He was, in His earthly body. He would have been partially guilty of the sins of His ancestors who worshipped graven images. Yet God is *'a jealous God, visiting the iniquity of the fathers upon the children to the third and fourth generations of them that hate* [Him]' (Exodus 20:5). Jesus did not trace His identity in a human father but in God. So His source of power on earth was not Abraham, Jacob, Isaac, David etc., it was God, His inheritance. God is our Father too, because Jesus did invite those who would join Him to become children of God. So, in Jesus we, like Him, have the privilege of by-passing all genetic inheritance.

When we believe we are accepted into Christ and by this means we become like Christ, whose Father is God. The word father means 'the one in whom you trace your identity'. Our earthly parents are obedient servants of God, carrying out the role of parent on God's behalf. It also makes no sense to talk about my parents' religion as if it were my own. You do not inherit a religion with your birth. In eternal terms what matters is God. I love my children. I have authority over them. But in heaven they will no longer be my children. They will be, as believers, children of God. If Celia and I were to die tomorrow, no-one should be crazy enough to make us into two new gods to bow down to, St Celia and St Simeon.

This revelation of who my true father is came as we approached the two rivers running side by side. We now had to cross the rivers, without walking through them, but my body could not do this. The angel, being a heavenly body, had no problem with this at all. I was provided with a kind of pad to stand on.

We were going to where Jesus was. He was inside an office. Outside I saw trillions and trillions of people waiting outside. We were in a part of paradise where Jesus was dealing with the affairs of men on earth; He was allocating them certain duties for their time on earth. It resembled a city. They worshipped as they waited. As Jesus entered the room to attend to His business they stopped worshipping and eagerly jostled with each other for the slimmest opportunity to talk to Jesus. Their problem was 'How can I show Him I really love Him?' They were in heaven, they could even see Jesus, but they had not been able to say it face-to-face, person-to-person. The majority of the people I saw were women. What surprised me was that they were dressed in every colour and style of modest clothing, which for the majority was not white. It seemed you had the choice of what to wear. The first man I saw was a long way away from meeting Jesus. He was a thousand miles away at least, in our terms. I know you will not like to read that. This man had repented, but instead of doing God's work, he had spent most of his time on earth nursing his grudges against his enemies. He had spent time cursing them, but now he was changing.

In eternity things didn't happen hour by hour in a sequential orderly fashion. They happened when they happened. There was no sense of time following time. This may not seem to make sense at first, but what seemed to have replaced the idea of time and clocks was the mind of Christ. Opportunities fell like fruit from the source of life, Jesus. When a fruit falls off a tree it is just a fruit. When it happens, it happens. And happy things always happened in this culture of ceaseless opportunities.

When we entered the room where Jesus was, I was surprised at how simple it all was. He was lying on a plain couch, and in a humble way, in simple surroundings, a very simple King, in a very simple and humble style. He looked up as if deep in thought. It was pleasing to see that He was personable in character. It kind of related to my humanity. I felt safe in His presence. The angel, who had guided me in, closed the door by leaning against it. The wood of the closed door was awesome. It had the beauty of eternity.

I was not alone. There were eight of us who stood before Jesus. It was absolutely lovely to be there. We felt an inexpressible sense of joy that pervaded our whole being. Jesus' presence did not give us any feeling of fear, in fact I felt like touching Him, and was just about to do so with my hand when the angel said, 'You are to ask one question each.'

Each of the eight of us was from a different country. We did not talk to each other or look at each other's faces. We were all focused on Jesus. The joy in our hearts was surely boundless. The sheer joy of being with Him there, with the One who was once crucified, put us all in a jubilant mood. Jesus Christ, yes, what awesome and eternal wonderment! Just remembering fills me with a perfect sense of the well-foundness of our belief in God. Yes, it validates all those loud passionate preachers on earth. Jesus is not some vague idea. He is not like an out of focus photograph. He is real. He is here. He was here, and we were here too, what an experience!

I was standing closest to Jesus' head and nearest to the angel as well, so I felt really special. What cheap, earthly, proud emotion. I thought I was freer than others to do what I wanted. I told Him about the ugly political situation in Uganda, and finished by asking if there was anything I could do to make a difference, 'What more, my Lord, have I not done?' He told me there were two others in the country whose preaching and style of life were all wrong and that I was to go and tell them that they were to change or He would kick them out of every place they would go. Naturally I am not going to name them. That information should remain private. However, I did go and see them and they rejected my message and have ended up kicked out from place after place. Their spiritual life has been drained away and is now an emaciated shadow of their previous success, because of their commitment to gain and dishonesty and other wickedness. Soon I was to see that I was no better than they. I wasn't wicked, dishonest or greedy, but I did not obey the angel's instruction carefully enough. I felt like Jesus had not quite answered me, so I tried to put the question another way. This was wrong. In heaven you must do exactly whatever Jesus tells you to do. The angel shouted a rebuke at me in the loudest sound that my ears had ever heard. It was a sound to wake the dead. No dead thing on earth could hear that sound and not resurrect! Now I can understand how God's Word can call all things that are not as if they are. His Word has absolute power over life and death. 'You were told only to ask one question!' Before he finished the sentence I was outside the room, feeling very ashamed of myself. I felt bewildered, like a suddenly resurrected rotten dog. Now what for this wretched dog, Simeon? But soon the angel joined me again and patted me on the back in such a friendly, comforting way that it was as if nothing had happened between the two of us only a moment ago. I noticed that in heaven no-one keeps grudges. Heaven seeks to restore everyone to good soil. Unlike in hell, heaven does not let anyone writhe in pain. What a glorious culture.

Now we were next to the two rivers again. Heavenly servants dipped their cups into the river of milk and gave them to those who had a particular calling on their lives. I was given one of these cups to drink. It tasted so good. The angel explained that unlike on the earth where milk comes from a cow's udder, here in heaven the milk flowed from the Word of God, giving life.

Think of a child born in Sweden. He has never seen a cow.

You ask him, 'Where does milk come from?' then he smartly gives his honest answer, 'from the fridge!' We too think that things come from things we know on earth. We think life comes from medicine, money from labour and votes from campaigns. But now I know better. Jesus said, *'It is written, "Man shall not live by bread alone, but by every word that proceeds from the mouth of God"'* (Matthew 4:4). That means that life comes from God. Yes, just as God said, milk comes not from a cow's udder but from God's Word.

Next I saw something very important. A man was trying to drink from the river of water but was unable to. Every time he tried the river just turned to mud. I asked the angel why that was.

'He has been brought here for your sake,' he replied, 'His name is Abdu. You will meet him in the next few days. He is not a believer in the Lord Jesus Christ, so he has no share in the kingdom of God. He is a very sick man when he is on earth and is being treated in one of the hospitals in your country and is about to die. He will be brought held in arms into your fellowship in four days. You will pray for him that he may live. Baptise him Joshua, for no-one has any share in the kingdom if he is not baptised. Go and tell the people before it happens so that when it does happen they will know that you have been here.'

When he said this I looked round me more intently so as to enjoy where I was. The wind we were breathing was life itself. It seems to me that the oxygen we breathe on earth is just the counterpart of the life we breathed in heaven, and cigarette smoke the earthly equivalent of the obnoxious miasma of smoke rising from the fiery valley of hell. The weather in heaven was kind to my skin as well as being so invigorating. There was something soothing and healing about the atmosphere. The angel and I talked about the things that happened both before and after the fall of man. 'This place is so beautiful, I want to stay here,' I said.

Just then, by God's power I was looking down on Namirembe Christian Fellowship. The place looked somewhat ugly and primitive. I had second thoughts about what I had just said to the angel. Celia's face came to mind. We had only been married for four years. My church members were going through a critical period of spiritual infancy. Millions had not yet heard what Jesus had sent me to do. 'If I do not go back, the people on earth will feel very bad.'

We walked on towards the place where we had landed after flying across the fires of hell. Before we reached the fires, suddenly a white light flashed across my eyes and down onto the earth. I was extremely petrified. I was relocated back into my body as easily as a film is reloaded into a camera. What a story I had to tell. It was even more dramatic than my first encounter with Jesus at the school when I was teaching. I told Celia first, then my church the following evening. At that time we used to meet to worship every night at Namirembe Christian Fellowship.

'That you may know that there does exist a heaven and that I myself walked there, the man I saw, Abdu, will be brought here in four days. You will see him and know that I am God's servant and that I am talking and acting from Him.' It was as if I was speaking a new language I felt so full of faith. I do not ever before remember having had my faith so increased as on this occasion. It felt like all the heavenly beings were ready to explode 'Go on, speak out!' at each word I spoke. It's a wonderful feeling to be speaking about something I knew so well.

I am not sure whether I died or not. I know I had left my body. If I did actually die, then I can reassure you that if you die in Christ there is a body safe for you waiting for you to live in it. Death is not the end. There is a life beyond death. You will not be in any pain or sorrow there. When you get there you will not want resurrection on earth or to return there. Although you do not want to die while you are here, when you finally do so it will be real success for you as a believer. The Bible teaches,

> *'Behold, I tell you a mystery: We shall not all sleep, but we shall all be changed – in a moment, in the twinkling of an eye, at the last trumpet. For the trumpet will sound, and the dead will be raised incorruptible, and we shall be changed. For this corruptible must put on incorruption, and this mortal must put on immortality. So ... shall be brought to pass the saying that is written: "Death is swallowed up in victory."'*

(1 Corinthians 15:51–54)

The fourth day after my bold prophecy was a great evening. People flocked into the fellowship like water over the rapids of the Nile. The church was packed. I had never seen it so full. It was almost filled to capacity. Our church building was nothing special to look at, just flimsy reed walls with a corrugated iron roof. The floor was not cemented and the dirt was covered with papyrus reed mats or old carpets. An old radio provided amplification for my voice, accompanied by the sickening howls of microphone feedback. Everybody was waiting anxiously to see whether the prophecy would come to pass or not, whether their belief was justified or not. I preached about miracles, power and strength from Mark 16:17. 'Believers are given the power to work miracles!' I declared boldly.

Right in the middle of my sermon an old man was brought in, a very tiny, sick, miserable looking man, carried in someone's arms just as I had prophesied. They put him down right in the middle of the church in front of the entire amazed congregation.

'There is the man!' I shouted from the pulpit. 'His name is Abdu. Ask him. Whatever you want to say, say it now!'

When the man confirmed his name was indeed Abdu, everyone went crazy. Tears ran freely down the cheeks of sinners repenting. Hundreds gave their hearts to Jesus that day. Abdu is a Muslim name. He had been brought from the Rubaga Catholic Missionary Hospital one-and-a-half miles away from Namirembe Christian Fellowship, but had not been baptised.

'He has been brought here for your sake,' they said.

Abdu, they all remembered the story. 'He will be brought into the fellowship in four days. Say it before it happens so that when it happens they will believe.'

Waiting hell, waiting heaven

It may seem a long time to us between Jesus' first coming and His final return. Sooner or later this prophecy will be fulfilled. We do not know the exact date when this will be, but we had better believe it will happen. There is a hell and a heaven waiting. The judgement day for all mankind will come and every single person who rejects Christ today will stand before God in final judgement for their lives. There really is a hell and heaven waiting for us today. The present hell will, together with the sinners it contains, be thrown into an even worse place called the lake of fire. There they will meet their eternal punishment.

> *'And He said to me, "It is done! I am the Alpha and the Omega, the Beginning and the End. I will give of the fountain of the water of life freely to him who thirsts . . . I will be his God and he will be My son."*   (Revelation 21:6–7)

Chapter 5

Seeing through God's Eyes

Let me speak freely now. There is a hive of activity behind the natural world you see. Outside the physical world you perceive with your five senses is a battlefield. Invisible forces are constantly engaged in powerful warfare that most people are totally unaware of. This conflict influences both world events and the day-to-day matters of individual lives, who to marry, plans for the future etc. We are the central focus of this war, whether we are aware of it, or believe it or not, so it is important for us to be informed. I think it is so important that the whole world should be aware of this fact.

You behave the way you do, and take paths you should have avoided, because you are dominated or influenced by driving forces beyond yourself. I call such forces strongholds. They are not only strong; they also fiercely take hold of us until we are subjected to their full authority. You should have a very clear picture from the last chapter that he who wishes to subject you to his authority so you may end up in the fire belt, is extremely wicked and evil. Yet the world is totally unaware that fallen angels, called demons, and Satan are doing exactly that. He will make sure that you identify only with the earthly attraction and remain unaware of the eternal price tag, the high price to be paid for temporal gain. Satan will make it appear as if those who identify with Christ are fools. We had all better know what we are doing. Remember what it looks like when you are standing on the edge of that cliff, looking down into that belt of fire. At the edge, every departing soul knows that the wisdom of sinners becomes foolishness at that critical cliff. This is no small matter. We are limited to the world of the five senses, and because we are such prime targets, we cannot do without Jesus' power to shatter demonically inspired mental deceptions or strongholds.

Because evil angels are engaged in heavenly battle against us, we often get into satanically stimulated arguments designed to destroy, or hinder our faith, and nullify God's blessings. For example, an inner false belief implanted by Satan can create doubt as to whether God is really who the Bible says He is. One single thought can make a big difference in a person's life. By a single thought a man can rape his daughter. Or a wealthy man can build a home for the physically handicapped. There is competition between God and Satan for possession of the hearts of human beings. Each time a baby is born, a destiny is formed under the influence of this clash of arguments, this relentless tension between noble ideals and shocking incidents. The way we take depends on the choices we make. It is entirely up to us to make whatever choice we wish to, but our choice will mould not only our own personal destiny, it will also affect our civilisation. The apostle Paul counsels us not to fight relying on our own senses alone, but on the weapons that God has designed for us, to have the might to pull down strongholds. When ugly, disbelieving thoughts are under control, we have a pure, quiet and renewed mind ready to receive the truth in faith. We are free to interact with the goings-on behind the senses, to walk comfortably a life that pleases God, to walk in the Spirit. Only this way can we accept the impartation of the power of God and develop a true and meaningful companionship with Him.

Personality revolution a must

If you want to receive miracles, power and strength, you must change. You must deal with yourself in a most thorough way.

You must forsake and forswear any rigid rules of culture if they construct a roadblock to your free access to your Heavenly Father. Culture is not inborn it is learned behaviour. Whatever has been learned can be unlearned. Faith in Jesus is a call, a war cry for a cultural revolution where men are to be transformed completely, to become a new creation.

It is absolutely possible to become a different person. No-one stays the same as the day they were born. We are all constantly changing, whether we are aware of it or not. In relating to others we cannot help upgrading or downgrading ourselves. We are constantly doing this, whether knowingly or unknowingly. If you do not change into God's children, circumstances or the devil will mould you into their desired person. There is no question about this. Only God does not change. We speak other people's languages, learn to eat their type of dishes, like their likes and hate their hates.

I come from a background of political turmoil, military take-overs and civil strife. The situation escalated into full-scale insurrection at one point and brought dangerous dictators including Idi Amin to power. Uganda bore the shame of being ruled by illegal, arrogant dictators whose political motivation was to exercise total power over a most unwilling, fatigued and cursing people. These dictators were like child molesters, vicious, full of heinous greed, fake medals decorating their chests. Intimidation of Ugandans, by the bloodshed of innocent people, was the source of their power and strength in which they took political pride. And just when we could not cope any more, war erupted. Ugandans from every level of society breathed and chanted rebellion, bloodshed and conflict. Weak, strong, rich, poor, sick, old men, women and children, all were rude. They were going to fight it out come what may. When they developed such an impolite attitude, a change took place. It had become a vicious cycle of violence. People waged war against their arrogant, ruthless, self-appointed rulers one after another, so throne by throne, each was pulled down in turn. The names changed but the corrupt culture stayed the same. When we change, the situation around us will change. If we don't change, the situation remains the same. Our family, health, country, continent, race, tribe, what have you, all will stay the same. If we are able to change for our own good, why don't we? Why don't the weak say, 'I am strong!'?

It's relatively easy to take the man out of the ghetto, but so difficult to take the ghetto out of him. If he does not re-adjust to his new surroundings, sadly there will be no difference between him now and him yesterday. In the same way, if we are not ready to be strong, it is no use to claim that by joining Jesus we become new creatures. The new nature must be seen in our thinking and in our actions, not just holiness. If all that was required were holiness, then Jesus would not have needed to come. The Pharisees, Sadducees and scribes knew more than enough to teach about holiness. God wanted man to change not only into holy disciples, but also into firm, unyielding, courageous and valiant children of God. The nature of God that was in Jesus was assigned to our lives as well. Those who join Jesus, the Bible says, were given the right to be children of God.

In my case, I knew in December 1977 that God had called me to wage war against my own ghetto nature, so that braced with the new nature of Jesus I was to defeat that deadly, ruthless, fallen angel, Lucifer. Lucifer is a supernatural being, but he is not the only supernatural being exercising authority on earth. He is not even the only angel here. The angels who defeated him and had him thrown down from heaven are assigned to minister for us who are heirs of salvation.

> *'Are they not all ministering spirits sent forth to minister for those who will inherit salvation?'*   (Hebrews 1:14)

We who have inherited the faith and power of Jesus are

enabled to do His works because we are ministered to by angels. But in order to fight him we have to be more than just men. We need to take on the nature of children of God. Only when we acquire God's nature can we tap into the supernatural. Only then is our faith going to be validated. When we are children we fight for our Father jealously. Then men had better stop fighting and insulting God in our presence! This was the right way, in true faith, it was that correct attitude that launched me into ministry.

Children of God are meant to be giants. They are meant to tower over other human beings. The first 'spoilt children of God' were giants. They were spoilt but powerful. Jesus came to teach us how to be the good acceptable children of God. But all in all, children of God cannot be weaklings.

> '... the sons of God saw the daughters of men, that they were beautiful: and they took wives for themselves of all whom they chose. And the LORD said, "My Spirit shall not strive with man forever, for he is indeed flesh; yet his days shall be one hundred and twenty years." There were giants on the earth in those days, and also afterward, when the sons of God came into the daughters of men and they bore children to them. Those were the mighty men who were of old, men of renown.'
>
> (Genesis 6:2–4)

> 'But as many as received Him, to them He gave the right to become children of God, to those who believe in His name.'
>
> (John 1:12)

I dropped my shyness, my fear of risk, my feelings of inadequacy, in order to pull down the strongholds of Satan. All these former attitudes became irrelevant. When, like old friends from the ghetto, beliefs from my family tradition or borrowed from my culture sneaked into my Christian life, I shrugged them off because this was a different time. It was a time of war, not of peace, but of noise, explosives and smoke. It was a time of iron on iron.

All who serve the supernatural should have elements of the supernatural. They must appear to be children, soldiers of the supernatural, all-powerful God who holds the universe together and who causes things to be. I was called to be a shepherd of the sheep. I had to bring them back to Him. So I had better stop being weak. It was a time of iron on iron, and because it was, I had to undergo an internal change. It does not matter how small I am in size, how insignificant I look to the outward glance. People do not follow the outward appearance. People were craving for someone with inner might, someone who spoke valiantly, not a drowning man's voice, a voice throbbing with the power of God. Not a John the Baptist in hides, but a powerful, beckoning, Spirit-filled voice of John the Baptist, even though in the wilderness! People had to see me as that. Then they would believe me and follow me. The devil had to face danger if he was to engage in warfare against me. Then he would know that he has no choice but to flee. Why would anyone flee unless he realises he is in danger? In Acts 19:14 the sons of Sceva who were not yet changed went ahead and preached but had a really rough time.

Change is so very important. If we are not thoroughly transformed we cannot effectively serve God. One has to be a new creation in order to work God's work. God's will is for us to be like Jesus in every way. This is not only about the human Jesus. God wants us to be like His Son, not a picture of His human conduct, but witnesses imbued with the supernatural power of Jesus' resurrection. His Word says in Malachi 3:6, *'I am the Lord, I do not change.'* The same miracle-working God who healed the sick, cast out demons and raised the dead expects us by the power of the Holy Spirit to uphold the same standards. That way people will understand that God does not change.

> *'And these signs will follow those who believe: In My name*
> *they will cast out demons; they will speak with new tongues;*
> *they will take up serpents; and if they drink anything deadly, it*
> *will by no means hurt them; they will lay hands on the sick,*
> *and they will recover.'*   (Mark 16:17–18)

In other words believers will be given the power to perform miracles. Whenever God sends a man to be His servant, He not only requires him to change his character, but He also wants him to act in an unnatural way, such as to perform miracles. By our mere fleshly ability we cannot fulfil such a noble requirement. Yet it is not God's duty to change us. It is our decision to change since He has given us the power to do so.

In our natural state we normally have a feeling of weakness, fearfulness and timidity but God has not given us these feelings. According to His will, He expects us to be more than conquerors, using non-carnal weapons, and to be full of love, power and a sound mind (2 Timothy 1:7). So I changed my prayer style from words of weakness to power-charged ones. 'If I am preaching Your Name, Lord, I say You are Almighty and Master. Prove this, my Lord, so that the world may know that I am speaking of the same God as Moses and Elijah spoke about. Answer me, O Lord, that the world may know that You are all mighty.' That is how I would pray.

Joshua

In the Bible Joshua was the successor to the great prophet Moses. It was hard for anyone to inherit the mantle of such a great man as Moses. When he decided to depend upon God's power he was able to obtain that real courage, maturity, leadership and miracles by which he reigned over Israel for twenty-five years, and acquired his legendary name. When you change, the situation around you changes too. You can change a whole country if you shift from a position of weakness to a

position of strength. Joshua started as a weak, trembling
man. Before he changed, the Israelites remained weak. When
he changed, they did too. Without changing you will never
make any impression on earth. You will never be a winner.
Weaklings are either turned into slaves or relegated to the
background of society. Our war against Satan is not a magic
war in which somehow the weaklings will defeat the strong.
We are called to be brave soldiers whose courage shall melt the
hearts of wicked men.

> *'Moses My servant is dead. Now therefore, arise ... No man
> shall be able to stand before you all the days of your life; as I
> was with Moses, so I will be with you.'*   (Joshua 1:2, 5)

Knowing God's Word was not all God sent Joshua to do. He
sent him to apply it effectively in actual life situations. There
are many people who know the Word of God by heart and can
recite every smallest detail accurately, but Jesus has not sent
them to do that. He has sent them on a tangible mission, not
just to recite words through the microphone to the church
building. We have been sent to agonising people, not to
stained glass windows. Our hands must heal cancer, AIDS,
headaches, heartaches, heart attacks, deep inner wounds,
fears etc. The Word of God is not just soothing psychology.
Jesus said 'You do it', 'You figure them out'. I agree!

How do you know that a miracle will happen?

In 1988 James Nabongo had been having some trouble at
home. Strange things had been happening in his house under
the influence of evil spirits. Things had been moving around
and several fires had started without explanation. On my
advice he took authority over the invisible powers that had
been causing the disturbances. He was a prominent member
of the Anglican Church, so following this deliverance, the

Bishop invited me to the diocesan meeting. There I was asked
to accept the title of rabbi to the church and to become a
member of the staff with responsibility for a new ministry of
the miraculous. The theme of the meeting was 'the general
concern about the atrophy of their church membership'. The
decline had occurred as the Namirembe Christian Fellowship
came into being. They asked me to advise their church on
how to increase their membership. When the Bishop called
upon me to speak, I expressed my appreciation for this topic
at a time when all children of God needed to be united in
order to raise the banner of our Lord. I also advised the church
to return to the teaching of the Scriptures. The Lord would
surely work miracles in the church. I turned down the job
offer of Anglican Church Rabbi, but offered to help the church
wherever I could. I told the Bishop, 'It is faith in Jesus, not my
feelings. I believe what I read, so I act.' I look at problems the
way Jesus would and I solve them the way Jesus would. This is
what faith is to me. I identify the feelings that I believe Jesus
feels concerning the matter set before me. I know that even
though I work for Him, it is still Him who works it out after all
is said and done. Since He cannot be defeated, I am not bound
to fail either.

I remember how Jesus felt, hurting His mother and His
dear friends by making the decision to be humiliated and die
a political traitor's death on a Roman cross for the sake of
those of God's people who were not even yet born. I get
moved to act for them if they are in trouble. When I
remember His miracles or the day that Jesus first spoke to
me, it feels like I am injected with love and victory over Satan
and diseases.

How to become a part of a miracle

When Jesus reveals something to me in a vision or a dream, I
will be obedient and do what Jesus has asked me to do. I will

play my part in His desired miracle. Usually a believer who performs these miracles has a close relationship with Jesus. In the Bible such believers were called prophets, teachers, apostles, evangelists, pastors, disciples and elders. The Lord also promised the prophet Joel:

> *'I will pour out my spirit on all flesh; and your sons and daughters shall prophesy, your old men shall dream dreams, your young men shall see visions: And also upon the servants and upon the handmaids in those days will I pour out my spirit. And I will shew wonders in the heavens and in the earth ...'* (Joel 2:28–30 AV)

His miraculous power was promised to young and old. The Bible reports that God anointed Jesus with the Holy Spirit and power that resulted in His ability to heal the sick and free them from demonic oppression. Sometimes this anointing is called baptism in the Spirit, which hits an individual during worship or preaching. At such a time, the individual is able to perform a miracle while the Spirit is working in him or her. This anointing changes the way a person feels, behaves and operates.

During worship or praise we feel a deep inflowing of life. The Spirit of God bubbles forth within us, refreshing us like the river of life gushing out of heaven and wending its way through us to bless, refresh and heal those around us. It's difficult to describe this feeling adequately, but it brings such vitality. We often experience this feeling just before a miracle is about to happen. It is a sign to us that God is about to work in the miraculous, either in our own life or to do a miracle for someone else. Often I will be reminded of the emotion attached to a situation, which will indicate in what way Jesus desires to work. For example, compassion like before the raising of Lazarus, or anger, like when Jesus overturned the moneychangers' tables at the temple, or appreciation of faith, when the woman who had the issue of blood. During these times I know what miracle He is going to do.

Seeing through God's eyes

When we live a faith-filled life, we learn to judge spiritual things by spiritual standards, the same way as God does, rather than by appearances as the world does. When we look with God's eyes, not just at the diagnosis in front of us, we are focused on Jesus' words for the situation. God does not expect us to stay looking through the world's mindset, through fleshly, carnal thinking. God expects us to have a believing heart of faith towards Him to perceive His mindset about the situation. Carnal man does not understand the things of the Spirit, they are foolishness to him. We are called to see things through God's eyes.

> *'For those who live according to the flesh set their minds on the things of the flesh, but those who live according to the Spirit, the things of the Spirit ... But if the Spirit of Him who raised Jesus from the dead dwells in you, He who raised Christ from the dead will also give life to your mortal bodies through His Spirit who dwells in you.'*   (Romans 8:5, 11)

When Peter stepped out of the boat and started walking on the water of the Sea of Galilee, he took the first steps successfully because he was looking at the situation through God's eyes. As long as he remained focused that way Peter did well. When he weakened in attitude and began to consider the impossibility of the situation, he began to sink. When we see through God's eyes we are open to the fullness of the Spirit and to His miracles.

When I had my out of the body experiences, one of the things I especially noticed was that the air that I breathed in heaven was purer than the air we breathe here on earth. The air there is life itself. It is that life that will flow like a river, flowing for the healing of the nations. The tree, which stands next to the river of life, bears twelve sorts of fruit. It draws water for its sap from the river. The Bible promises that those who believe in Jesus will have rivers of living water flowing out of their hearts (John 7:38). Some translations say 'life-giving water'. We can drink this life giving water from Jesus.

> *'Jesus stood and cried out, saying, "If anyone thirsts, let him come unto Me and drink."'* (John 7:37)

Jesus was given this anointing of power and the Holy Spirit and He went around healing the sick and freeing the demon oppressed (read Acts 10:38). Those who thirst for the power that gives life can ask Jesus to send to them the Holy Spirit and anointing by which they will do well. We too can inhale this life while we are on the earth – that is if we will see things Jesus' way. We can also give this life to others. That is why Jesus breathed on the disciples and said, *'Receive the Holy Spirit'* (John 20:22). Jesus also said to them *'Peace to you! As the Father has sent Me, I also send you'* (John 20:21). When Jesus said this, healing power and miracles gushed into their life. Healing gushed into their life. The healing power of Jesus came into the disciples as a breath.

When Joshua was called to lead Israel, he received God's power for the task. It was heaven's breath he received. When a man's life is breathed on by God, it changes him so he is strengthened and changed to view things as God sees them. God knows you can be totally changed. To change means to become totally different. You no longer behave the same way you once did. With new input you think entirely differently.

When God changed Joshua, he became a stronger person than he had ever been. He had none of the usual scepticism most people have about faith in God. There was no suspicion of God. Does it make any difference, you might ask me, whether you like the idea of faith in God or not? Joshua certainly knew it makes a great deal of difference. I believe Joshua was aware of some of the skills of a stonemason. He knew when facing Jericho that stone walls do not just crash to the ground, but he believed it when God spoke and told him the walls would come crashing down without the aid of tools. Faith can be stronger than the tools of a stonemason. Joshua learned from being with Moses what God could do. God expects our faith to do something (Hebrews 11:6). It's not just for fun. It's to meet real needs by carrying out duties delegated from heaven. It means fulfilling the same purpose as the angels, ministering to needs on the earth. Angels are not just doing things for the sake of it. If anyone thinks angels do miracles just for fun, he does not know what he is talking about. Angels have very serious assignments to carry out. In the same way, believers should understand what Jesus expects them to do for Him. Learn from Jesus whose tasks are easy (Matthew 11:28–30).

Joshua's first duty was to cross the Jordan River without the aid of a bridge or any technology. The waters would part to allow the Children of Israel to walk across the dry riverbed. His life's assignment was to include the crashing down of Jericho's walls through sheer faith and the conquering of thirty-one kingdoms, demonstrating defeat of their pagan gods. All he had for soldiers was a nation of tired slaves' children to set against the well-fed trained armies. God's only provision for Joshua was the change of character in order to tap into the formidable resources of heaven. If Joshua obeyed God by observing His Word, He would give him every place the sole of his foot would tread upon (Joshua 1:3). If he kept God's law, no man would be able to withstand him all the days of his life (Joshua 1:5), only he was to be strong and of good courage.

God spoke to Joshua *'Moses My servant is dead ... now there-fore ... go.'* In other words, it was as if God had said, 'I know you have this pain of bereavement. You are mourning and your heart is aching. The Israelites are mourning and in addition they are afraid of all these warrior nations they are facing. They need someone like Moses, someone who can order nature to obey God's will, someone who can subdue a whole empire using a stick, someone who can do creative miracles like making a real snake. Joshua, you have to stand up and be strong!'

Like you, inside Joshua faced fear. But Joshua made that decision to wake up and say, 'Alright, I'm going to be strong and show the world what God has told me to be. I will show the wicked kings of these thirty-one kingdoms what God has said to me.'

What does it mean to be strong? It means being courageous. That means even if it looks risky to make some assertions or to take certain actions, do not be afraid. Don't even think about being afraid, don't be afraid of being ashamed. If God wants us to heal the sick, don't be discouraged if you pray for some people and they die. They would have died anyway. Even if ten should die in a row when we first start, being strong means that you don't give up before you have started. It means taking no notice if other people think that is too risky. A hospital doesn't shut down just because one patient has died. If you give up you are just giving in to Satan. Why should he weaken you? If three people were cured of AIDS or cancer, it would justify all the other instances where no miracle occurred. Strong means to be manly, unshakeable, someone who can stand and plant the Lord's banner in a particular spot, whatever may come against him. It means to be unyielding. It means even if he should face setbacks, he is going to go forward into conflict because he is assured of victory. Triumph is the end result of displaying courage. So, Joshua, my boy, get up and go, says God *'Take courage.'*

Joshua had to learn to go forward, doing God's command without question. In John chapter 2 we read of the story of when Jesus turned water into wine at the wedding. The servants were perplexed about the process. How could He produce wine without grapes? The answer is in Jesus' way, not man's way. Thinking of Jesus' way makes me strong. I take Mary's words literally. *'Whatever He says to you, do it'* (John 2:5). Our way is different from His way. Believers are called to embrace His way, *'the way, the truth, and the life'* (John 14:6). To be effectively walking God's way Joshua was told to be courageous and strong, not to be weak, timid and fearful, like we often feel. God required him to change to doing everything God's way.

Today the prophetic call is the same. 'My servants the apostles are dead. Barbara, Celia, Simeon, go and be Moses! Be Peter, Paul or Daniel. Cancer victims, drug addicts, sinners, poor people, those oppressed by demons are crying out to Me.' How can you be called to heal cancer or AIDS and still not think you need to be strong? I don't think you can offer a valid excuse. I think it's what you need to fulfil what God expects of you.

Put on My yoke

Jesus sent His disciples to present His Word in the same way He did Himself. He sends believers with the power to work miracles and cast out demons. He also equips believers with His own nature, His character, meek and gentle. He says, *'Learn from Me, for I am gentle ... [put on my yoke]'* (Matthew 11:28–29). One of the wonderful aspects of the gospel is the ability for natural man to be able to kick out supernatural demons. Most people, most of the time, are not aware of these beings that cannot usually be detected by the senses, by sight, touch, smell, taste or hearing. Faith is the great wonder of my life. It lifts me high above the trials of everyday life. Like being in an aeroplane, it raises you far higher than you could have imagined and there exposes you to a whole new perspective. It reveals marvels far away from home. Faith involves you in spiritual battles with enemies that were around long before you were born. The searchlight of God reveals all this.

Demons really do exist. They are not just your own wicked thoughts, as some think. The following testimonies will give you much insight into their existence and ways of working. We will become aware we are not alone. Intelligent beings are all around us, some of them evil. We will wise up to Satan's will, desires and goals. Maybe the Kennedy Space Centre should not have spent so many millions of dollars looking for intelligence on other planets. So far they have only succeeded in bringing to earth a few blind pieces of rock. It's my opinion the money would have been much better spent on asking instead whether God, or even the devil, exists. When the astronauts return to earth, we are fascinated by the stories of their adventures. We get all excited and wait intently to hear what they have to say. Then they show us dead rocks. And they hold up their hands and say, 'Sorry, ladies and gentlemen, there is no life on the moon.' I'm sorry, hard working astronauts, there may not be life on the moon but I can show you plenty of life outside earth, just in case one day you want to go and live there. Let us look at some of the evidence of our adversary first.

Two friends of mine, members of the Anglican Church in Kampala, Mr James Nabongo and the other I will call Dr Nsu to maintain his privacy, faced active conflict with the devil. On July 19th 1987 Dr Nsu came from Mulago Hospital where he works, to see me, looking very miserable. I was sitting chatting to one of the Calvary Cross Choir members when he approached. He took me aside and asked for prayer following a frightening experience affecting his family. They had become quite petrified by the attentions of a witchdoctor. Dr Nsu was well educated, and had been the object of jealousy because he had gained the highest marks in his medical examination finals. A few of his fellow students were in the habit of consulting witchdoctors.

As we remember from Chapter 3, a witchdoctor is a priest dedicated to evil spirits, claiming to be the spirits of dead tribal heroes, who are able to tap into satanic power. With this power he is able to control natural objects or living things to harm people or perform counterfeits of God's blessing. People pay exorbitant fees for these witchdoctor's services. Jesus has authority over all works of witchcraft, including those who claim to be doing good things such as healing, giving wealth or protection.

For four weeks Dr Nsu had sensed that his home was under attack. On the day the exam results were announced things in his house started moving around by themselves. He would put a suit on a hanger in the wardrobe and watch it fly off and land on the floor in a corner of the room. The furniture also moved; it ended up all in a corner in a heap. He kept a big container of water in the house, as there was no tap. After drawing off one cup of water the rest mysteriously disappeared.

I was unable to visit straight away, but I promised to go to see him at 2 p.m. the following day, taking the Calvary Cross choir with me. As we approached the house we heard a loud thud. The devil heard us coming and revealed himself in this banging. We prayed and anointed the house with olive oil. Before we were even out of the place, the mess left the place. The doctor's friends thought he should have consulted the witchdoctor but Dr Nsu came to us instead.

A few months later Mr Nabongo's house was affected in a similar way. His house was in permanent chaos and he too was advised to seek the help of the witchdoctor. Because he was a believer in Jesus he of course would not do this. His wife told me he had even been advised by one of the Anglican clergy to consult a witchdoctor since the church did not have any solution to the problem. Fortunately he was a friend of Dr Nsu who had had a similar problem, who told him to come to me. So after three months of disturbance, which had been reported in the local paper, I was consulted.

Margaret and James had recently evicted a tenant who had left a week before the disturbances started. We believe she probably consulted a witchdoctor to get revenge for her harsh treatment. Margaret and James have never consulted a witchdoctor themselves, and belong to a church that denies the existence of a personal devil or that demons can cause such things as they experienced. They believed before this happened to them that the devil was just an expression of our own nature that inclines us to do evil things, not a spiritual being that could cause actual physical harm.

James described the situation as a mystery of mysteries. His belongings flew out of the windows by themselves and landed up scattered all around the compound. Next all the glass started to shatter, including the dressing mirror and the windows. Splinters of glass were found in their food. Whenever the family sat down to eat they would be picking glass out of their tea or porridge. Margaret showed me three piles of clothes that had been damaged by fire, including the children's school uniforms. There was also a collection of plastic bottles, basins, buckets etc that had also been burned. Any item that had been bought new, or even if they were brought into the house to look at, would end up in this state. Invisible forces would cause sparks of fire to appear and damage the things. Cups flew out of the cupboards all by themselves. There was even a burnt hot pepper container lying on the floor next to the boy's quarters, its contents spilled, which Margaret said had come crazily out of the pantry and hit her mother-in-law.

We got the distinct impression there were invisible hands throwing these things all around, causing chaos. They would rudely pick up things all over the house and throw them around. No-one who saw that house could deny the existence of the devil. We simply sat down and ordered the mess to cease. And that was that.

James and Margaret regularly tell their story. They are convinced that they saw a great deliverance that day. They still live in Lukuli village, on the eastern outskirts of Kampala, Uganda. They are proud to testify to Ugandans and to foreign visitors what God has done. They invite visitors, especially from the UK or USA, to see for themselves. They want the world to know what Jesus can do today. They have a whole village of neighbours who can verify that this really happened.

Through these two examples we confirmed that beyond the natural realm we see the invisible world of spiritual forces is actively engaged in warfare. These forces not only move things around in houses, they also manipulate marriages, our health and our finances and have influence over many aspects of our lives. There is no immunity for those who do not believe in such things. They are affected even if they deny it.

The bishop of Margaret's church attended one of our services at Namirembe Christian Fellowship. Margaret Nabongo gave her testimony. She was a grandmother, she explained, an adult of maturity, and not a liar. She was pleased to testify and try as he might, he could not deny the reality. Margaret's church denied the possibility of personal interference by evil spirits, but she was very happy to share her experience in front of someone who knew her well from her old church.

One of my choir member's mothers is a practising witch-doctor. This choir member rejoices that Jesus has rescued her. Her family has suffered a great deal from the devastating things that have happened to them. She says it's so nice to feel that she is held in the safe hands of God.

I know that those who downplay the power of Jesus and that of our enemy the devil in their theology are wrong. They are acting in ignorance. In the unseen world there is a God who still does miracles, **if** we believe. The Bible is not talking of a state of mind when it talks of Satan, neither was Jesus talking of an inactive Christianity when He sent His disciples out to the nations. He told them to exercise real power by demonstrating the miraculous. When Jesus commissioned the church in Acts 1:8, He sent believers into actual supernatural phenomena. Satan has an army of fallen angels ready to attack anyone on any weakness, but the army of the Lord's angels will always overpower him in the name of Jesus.

Jesus ordered me to bring His people back to Him, to tell them to leave witchcraft and go back to Him. He promised to be with me wherever I went and to perform miracles and wonders as a testimony to those commands He gave me.

'But you shall receive power when the Holy Spirit has come upon you; and you shall be witnesses to Me . . . '   (Acts 1:8)

'And these signs will follow those who believe: in My name . . . '
(Mark 16:17)

It perplexes me to hear Mark 16:17–19 downplayed in intellectual circles nowadays, as if to imply that Jesus never quite promised the impartation of power to believers. They would almost rather call someone who does miracles a false prophet. That would really be turning the Bible message inside out, but would still end up proving my point, that the devil, which is the inspiration of the false prophet, really exists.

In the invisible realm believers have the power not only to do what was promised in Mark 16:17–19, but also do even greater works, works such as stopping the mouths of lions, subduing kingdoms, quenching the violence of fire, breaking stone walls, bringing prosperity to a believer's life and enabling believers to escape the edge of the sword. The gospel is not just a presentation of words. Heaven is on the alert to watch Jesus Christ being given all the glory on earth. The Father wants nothing apart from this, to see the Son glorified on the earth.

Chapter 6

Jesus the Great Physician

Jesus is on trial for giving people false hope, says the court of contemporary wisdom. Science, technology, philosophy and worldly thinking compile the prosecution case in this court. The alleged crime is that Jesus gives false hope by making false claims. The prosecution says Jesus is not the Saviour, He has no power and the devil does not exist. Yet Satan presents himself in this court as the prime speaker of the prosecution counsel. I appear for the defence and will prove Jesus 'not guilty' *'casting down arguments and every high thing that exalts itself against the knowledge of God'* (2 Corinthians 10:5). When I have finished my submission, and I am most sincere in this, I know that hope will be restored to the victims of those who contend against Christ. The highway of holiness will continue to be available for all who believe, to embrace the promise of eternal life.

We have developed too high an opinion of ourselves. We have become puffed up by our great achievements. Surely, it must be obvious to everyone that we are insufficient of ourselves. Is there a human on this earth to whom it is not obvious that while we may be very good at some things, there are others we are not able to do? Wisdom dictates that we admit there are many things we yet need to know. We need not get so puffed up.

Computers cannot detect demons, nor understand the power behind the wicked deeds people either knowingly or unknowingly inflict on each other. I have presented some evidence to show there are extra factors you have not always taken into account. You still know very little about some things. When scientists try to devise proof of extraterrestrial activity, using their computer programmes, so far this remains elusively unproven. Computers are still lacking when it comes to analysis of the spiritual realm. There is still a war going on that all our arsenal of nuclear weapons is no help at all in winning. It makes not a scrap of difference unleashing the biggest nuclear bomb against such a target. Indeed all our weapons of natural strength are useless against the battle going on against the powers of evil in the heavenly realm. Using carnal, earthly weapons against such an enemy is futile. I wish good luck to anyone attempting to subdue a demon with a nuclear bomb, or in any other way without God. If you can bring about your own return to life after your own death as Jesus did, then perhaps you do not need God. The single most amazing fact about Jesus is that after He died, not of natural causes, but by trauma, He came back to life three days afterwards. He rose from the dead on the third day! If anyone were able to do the same, he or she would need no God.

The idea has crept into society that the process of evolution makes us a self-made race. I consider such a view a miracle in itself. Even given a long time in which this development took place, I cannot imagine order coming out of chaos without a mind being involved in the process. Imagine the intelligence of a fireball moving very fast, and then cooling down, hardening into an atom at the same time. This is the heart of the Big Bang theory. How can such a complicated system as the human race, animals, oxygen and carbon dioxide arise out of nowhere? Whose idea was it to have a fireball spark off life? The Big Bang theory postulates that simple atoms combined into bigger ones, bigger atoms into molecules, and molecules into more complicated compounds. Rocks came out of heaps of molecules. Then vast continents followed, and on earth cells developed, and living organisms developed into species. Species modified into other species. Charles Darwin imagined the whole process taking millions of years to emerge. Nothing too drastic needed to occur in all that time, just a steady progression of survivable events, nothing to interrupt the smooth progression of order in Darwin's blessed, peaceful, cool millions of years.

Bright idea. How can a vastly complex system such as the planetary system, the earth with its interdependent ecology of plants and animals, be generated with no sensible origin? If I were to come home and find the house clean, the furniture neatly arranged, the television tuned to my favourite pro-gramme and dinner in the oven, and say all this happened by accident, how intelligent would this comment be? We could also ask, 'Howcome we do not see the process of chimpanzees turning into humans happening before our very eyes? What stopped the process? Why are there any apes at all? Why aren't they all human beings?' Scientists still cannot explain to me how something can appear out of nothing. What would happen if I sat down to a nice meal in a restaurant and then refused to pay the bill because I didn't see the chef who cooked it? Ignorance is no excuse. Because I did not see anyone, am I right to presume there is no chef? If I don't get away with that naiveté in the restaurant, that same argument does not hold water with the origin of life either. We have to avoid being so naïve. I will next tell the story of Frances Gill, a person who was healed, Darwin might have said by chance, or he might even have conceded healed by God, but a person who in the first place was created nevertheless by no-one!

Frances Gill's healing

As I write, a sparkling brunette, Kay Gill is sitting opposite me in her home in Lee on Solent. It's the 16th of August 2000. A plane flies close enough to us for us to see the pilot, Paul, waving to us before he lands at the Police Airfield. Kay is the wife of Andrew Gill who pastors a church in the town. My wife Celia, our secretary Barbara and I are staying for two days at the end of a two-month preaching tour of the United States and Great Britain. We are meeting to celebrate the healing of their daughter's arm. Frances had a deformed arm from when she was a baby. Kay, her mother, says the arm was either broken at birth or shortly after and the bones healed in incorrect alignment. She was now fourteen years old. Frances was unable to carry anything requiring both arms without dropping it and would often break things, or spill the contents if she tried, for example, to carry a bowl of water. When they saw the orthopedic surgeon, X-rays confirmed the bones were set in poor alignment but did not recommend operation as he they said it would be too traumatic and painful. The doctor suggested Frances should continue to live avoiding any sport that needed the use of this arm. 'I didn't feel happy and I was quite upset about it,' Frances said. The whole family had prayed for her healing many times. Kay says she had often asked God to heal her.

I first met the family in 1999 and we have become very deep friends of theirs, especially after the healing of their daughter. 'Very deep friends is an understatement', says Kay when reading the draft. Three weeks earlier I was preaching in the summer conference of C.net churches at Westpoint, near Exeter. This conference was of about 2,600 people and delegates attended from around forty different countries. After the service Frances asked me to pray that God would heal her. That night her healing began. The next day both Kay and Frances rushed up to me to testify to what had happened. In front of the large audience Frances stretched out her arm straight, like a cloth unfolding, as I held her hand and raised it before our Lord Jesus. Frances' doctor was reluctant to subject her to further pain and possible side effects. Jesus made it well without any anaesthesia, surgery or pain.

Jesus, the Great Physician

The great physician was a carpenter by the name of Jesus. Whilst on earth He lived in Cana of Galilee for some time. There was always a large crowd thronging round Him, making it difficult to get near Him. As you pressed forward, anxious to be close to Him, to enjoy the warmth of His presence, sometimes your faith would falter, as you found things rather different from what you expected. In fact He looked nothing like what you thought He would. Whatever great picture you had envisaged in your mind, His appearance was everything to the contrary.

Jesus was a plainly dressed man, a little dusty from walking on the road, a little travel weary even. How ridiculous to add my sorrow to what He already has to bear, but God had ordained that in this man was to be placed all His people's blessing. The sacred oracles were held in Him, for the salvation of all. It might distress you a little to realise what sort of simple lifestyle He kept. All the same, your own doubt could cost you dearly. It could even cost you your life.

The Healer was not a nobleman. He earned His own living in the small workshop that specialised in making boats for the fishermen who lived near the lake. Jesus was the eldest son of Mary, adopted by her husband Joseph, following the mysterious circumstance of His conception before His mother had had any physical relationship with a man. Jesus had inherited the workshop when He was twenty years old and as the eldest shouldered the duty to provide for the family. This was the stepping-stone for His public ministry. His first companions were former fishermen and tax collectors. Tax collectors were never far away from businesses, and were often to be found visiting Jesus' workshop. They also watched the fishermen closely. Peter, who lent Jesus his boat to speak from one day, had two problems. One of these was the taxman. After he joined Jesus this proved not so much of a problem after all. The second problem was the lack of fish and consequent business failure. This too Jesus sorted out, and Jesus would be a regular visitor to Peter's house. Because Peter allowed God into his home, his income increased and his mother-in-law was healed. There was a mighty secret in this plainly dressed man from Galilee. The carpenter was a healer. He says, *'I am the Lord who heals you.'*

A carpenter repairs wooden objects and structures. He can also be called a joiner. A joiner is a particularly skilled crafts-man who makes window and door frames and doors. We are all objects in His workshop, works in progress. Entering a church, the sound of the Holy Spirit working in our bodies is like going into a workshop where metal is being straightened out with a hammer. His touch makes our voices sing, our hips to gyrate, bodies to dance, now a waltz, then a rock and roll and our hands to heal. The Westpoint Sports Centre was noisy too, as Kay and Andrew checked their daughter's arm. Gathered round us were members of Southampton Community Church, Tony Morton's church on the south coast of England. It was amidst this chiselling, sawing and banging that we watched Frances' arm being healed. We were all swept into the whirl-wind of worship and praise as the bones blew back into shape.

This picture of the Divine Joiner encourages me whenever I am ill. The Bible tells us that creation happens when God shapes things by the power of His word.

> *'But now, O LORD, thou art our father; we are the clay, and thou our potter; and we are all the work of thy hand.'*
>
> (Isaiah 64:8 AV)

As an artist, I get very upset when I see a sculpture I have made damaged in any way. I immediately want to take my tools, the same ones I originally used to make it the first time, and restore it to its original beauty again. I am not detached about it in the slightest. Often we come to God as if bringing a broken sculpture to the Almighty Artist's studio. Whenever I see someone with a major problem, I am emboldened by my memories of a previous miracle and that is what I expect to see for the current situation.

In 1992 I suffered from thyrotoxicosis. I felt unwell, I lost a lot of weight and shook a lot, my eyes bulged and I sweated a great deal. The newspapers were on to this and cartoons of me appeared making fun of me by all sorts of captions. The papers were right; I did look very ugly. Skinny body, scrawny neck, I was not anyone's image of a handsome husband. I was amazed that Celia was so loyal to me. I expected my friends to shun such a freak. They would surely find it inconvenient to sustain a relationship with such a desperate looking fellow as I was.

However, I knew the Carpenter's commitment would not falter. He would set to work on opening shuttered lives. I turned to Him, my fellow artist, and He restored me miraculously. The Hebrew word *rapha*, 'to heal' also means 'to restore, repair and to mend'. Restoring particularly applies to muscles and repair to broken bones.

If an artist were to use himself often as a model for his painting or sculpture, it would reveal the depth of his love for himself. He loves himself so much that he recreates his own image. Suppose this artist were to print thousands of copies of his portrait and sell them all over the city, so every gallery, newsagent, office and library had a copy. It would be obvious that the man loved the artistic impression he had made of himself. It is so important to him that he has duplicated this picture over and over again. The artist does not rest until he is sure that the work he has done is a true reflection of the glow he has in his soul. His masterpiece is a source of his own glory. The closer the portraits come to the real appearance the happier he is, the more glory he gets. Because the picture comes from his own head, you can call it his own lovely son, his brainchild.

When God created man that is exactly what He did. He said, *'Let Us make man in Our image, according to Our likeness'* (Genesis 1:26). His glory is reflected in our likeness to Him. He made sure the environment was absolutely suited to man's needs. Everything was ecologically sound, no pollution no toxins, a perfect paradise. Then He gave the order, *'Be fruitful and multiply; fill the earth and subdue it; have dominion over . . . '* (Genesis 1:28). Just the same authority as God! According to God's plan, we are a reflection of God's self. If Satan should try to destroy this creation, he would come in for dire consequences because when he tries to destroy the creation he is offending the Creator. If he tries anything on with you, he is attacking God Himself.

When God heals and protects you, He is protecting Himself. In Matthew 25:40, Jesus says, *'inasmuch as you did it to one of the least of these My brethren, you did it to Me.'* If anyone gave to a beggar, he actually gave to Jesus; if anyone visited a sick person, he actually visited Jesus. Even more explicit are Jesus' words to Saul of Tarsus, on his way to Damascus to imprison and kill Christians,

> *' "Saul, Saul, why are you persecuting Me?" And he said, "Who are You, Lord?" Then the Lord said, "I am Jesus, whom you are persecuting. It is hard for you to kick against the goads." So he, trembling and astonished, said, "Lord, what do You want me to do?" Then the Lord said to him, "Arise and go into the city, and you will be told what you must do." '*
>
> (Acts 9:4–6)

The Authorised Version translates the word 'goads' as 'pricks'. Because all people are created in the image of God, when I look at an ill person, I see them as Jesus' body that the devil is trying to injure by inflicting them with a disease. A mere creature, a created being, he cannot successfully *'fight against the pricks'* of his own Creator. The pricks, I sense, are the words of God by which I am commanded to remove the works of Satan from human flesh.

'Arise and go into the city, and you will be told what you must do.' What does this mean to you? To me, it means that Paul did not know what he would be doing from then on. Paul could no longer make the decision about where to go, or what to do. He must wait for his orders and follow them. He would be told how and what to do. Following orders without understanding them means two things. You must know your boss, and stand before him to take your instructions.

When my wife Celia prepares a meal, she mingles her love for me with the preparation. When I eat, it is not just the bodily nourishment she is providing; I am also receiving her love. If I were to merely pick at the food, she would be hurt and say, 'Why did I take all that trouble?' In other words, 'Why do you not respond to my beacon of love?' So when I eat her meal, I am actually consuming the heart she put into it, not just food. It is not just a cup of coffee, or fruit juice, it is like a strong statement, a poetic explosiveness. It is a force that is meant to melt me. By her meals she reshapes me thoroughly. It is not a meal. It is a sweet smile. In the same way, when I accept the promise for my healing or any other miracle, I am responding to the love of Jesus who bled for me. By accepting His offer of a miracle, I make a decision to consume His love. When His love permeates my being it bandages and heals every wound in my soul, spirit and body. It is written in Isaiah 53:5 *'by His stripes we are healed.'*

Though we are only an image made in God's likeness, not God Himself, we are still appointed to do the things God does. Jesus says,

> *'Most assuredly, I say to you, he who believes in Me, the works that I do he will do also; and greater works than these he will*

> *do, because I go to My Father. And whatever you ask in My*
> *name, that I will do, that the Father may be glorified in the*
> *Son.'*   (John 14:12–13)

It is not far-fetched at all to be like Jesus. God has desired us to
be so. No longer are we to be like fallen Adam, we are to be like
Jesus. When Jesus humbled Himself and was baptised by John,
it appears the Father was beside Himself with joy. He interrupted the service. He just had to exclaim to those watching,
'This is My beloved Son, in whom I am well pleased' (Matthew
3:17). A voice came from heaven. It's as if the Father was
saying, 'Excuse me butting in on your religious service, that's
My SON!' Later the Son expects us to learn from Him.

Two-and-a-half years later the Son, that Son whom the
Father was well pleased with, was smashed and shattered on a
Roman cross. On the third day the Carpenter's, or Creator's,
skills came back into use again. On the third day, the Father
repaired the shattered body of His Son and made Him alive
again.

Because I am a trained artist, it is easy for me to produce a
work of art. But for someone who is not artistic, I can give
them a century to produce a painting and however hard they
try they will not create a masterpiece. What would take them
a year to do would take me twenty minutes. We should not
worry about how God is going to fulfil His promises to us; we
are not God. We do not have the power He has. The battle is
not ours. If we would only ask and believe, we will see what
God can do for us.

Never mind the evil army stationed behind the universe
waging war on us continually, God has His army of angels
fighting the rebellious, destructive fallen angels for the
human race. We are, in fact, the very focus of this unseen
conflict. God is proud of us. We are His workmanship, and
from the very beginning Satan was set on destroying what
God had made. Satan fights every good idea God stands for.

On the one hand a standing army of vicious intent, on the other Jesus has been revealed to us so that we might have life, abundant life (John 10:10). Jesus was revealed to us so that, through faith in Him, we may receive salvation and power to defeat every attack and oppression of Satan.

If we want to have a sound, joyful life, we must resist Satan by our faith in Jesus. The history of Israel is full of examples of amazing victories over the most frightening of situations, including the forces of nature. The parting of the Red Sea, Elijah's victory over the false prophets of Baal, the tumbling of Jericho's walls without a hand being laid on them, Samson's defeat of two hundred Philistines in one battle using the jawbone of an ass as his only weapon, are some of the examples we have already looked at. Satan can control nature to a certain extent. We can also affect the elements if they threaten our survival. Diseases come into this category and are therefore healed in Jesus' Name.

The wise, the strong, the intelligent and the rich are just as exposed to the invisible world of heavenly conflict as the less well endowed. Many people are aware of the fight and do take the appropriate action, but there are still too many who are unaware. Some remain unbelievers in spite of having witnessed a miracle. I want to paint the picture of the typical person who is unaware of the cosmic struggle. They often share this common mindset. He or she is agnostic or atheist and takes little interest in spiritual things. For such a person I am prepared to swear in a court of law that my testimony is true.

Yesterday, on the 24th of October 2000, Celia, my secretary Barbara and I were in a taxi travelling from Hounslow into the West End of London to join friends for dinner at a Lebanese Restaurant. The driver, who was Ghanaian, vehemently denied God's existence. 'What nonsense,' he said, 'I am my own god. I work hard to have a good life. I have made heaven for myself, heaven on earth. I am angry with my daughter who still goes to church. God and the story of Jesus dying on the cross is just a story made up by thieves. These unscrupulous preachers mislead people so they can drive around in Porsche cars. I heard that my daughter, who is nineteen, had been to see this pastor privately about some affair. I am going to look up this man's phone number and I am going to blast him.' He then changed tack, 'Where will I go if I am dead? Nowhere. When I am dead that's the end, finish. A dead man is finished, finished. What more? Witchdoctors are all thieves. I went to see many witchdoctors. I have swallowed five bullets, fetishes. A witchdoctor told me once that I would live until I am ninety-nine. They are all criminals and thieves.'

'How can you ever hope to get peace in your heart?' I asked him.

'I told you, I get peace when I work hard, that's all. My brother is a professional footballer here in the UK. My two daughters are both OK. Look at this photo of my son. That is my peace. My wife is in Ghana. I will go back to see her in December. And I have this foolish woman here in the UK, taking me to court claiming I am neglecting her! I have declared myself retired. I am clever; she won't get anything from me!

'I hate politicians, pastors, Africans, whites; they're all thieves. Even if you should become president of Uganda, with an honest heart and a good mind now, you will finally slide into wickedness and robbery. We are all thieves in a world of thieves. Do not lie to me; there is no God.' He even included the Prime Minister and Royal family in his curses.

I felt sad and desperate in my heart because I could not see any way I could share some of my experiences because he was so hardened. He was firmly convinced that all preachers are thieves and fakes. He thinks we just preach for the money, targeting the poor to take advantage of them. I couldn't even admit I'm a preacher. But I hope that some day he will read this book.

About a year after Celia and I were married, I was lying next to my lovely wife. It was around midnight and I began to detach from my body, which I could see still lying next to Celia on the bed. Light flooded over me and I was aware of, but could not quite see, an angel who sped me over the universe to heaven. We travelled at great speed over a stack of universes and entered heaven through a big gateway. I found myself standing in an important office in what seemed to be a huge administrative area. I noticed immediately that everything looked set ready for some meeting, but I couldn't guess what the purpose of the meeting would be. Maybe, I thought, it had something to do with obtaining instructions by which my life schedule was to be reset. I didn't even know if I would be returning to earth. I saw an angel dressed all in white, who looked at me with an air of authority. His look was extremely purposeful. He stood behind a large table that looked as though it had been made millions of years ago. As he was there waiting for me, I concluded he was there to execute some decision that had been taken at a previous meeting which I was not a party to. This was no occasion for flippant remarks, such as, 'Hi, good to see you.' Or pleasantries such as 'Let me hang up your jacket for you.'

'The reason you are here is to tell Ben he will die in one year.' That's not his real name. I won't publish that to avoid embarrassment to his family. So I will call the man Ben and his wife Millie. 'Come,' continued the angel. He led me to the room next door by an inner door on the left-hand side, while I walked via the hallway outside and stood outside the outer door. He called me in to explain the decision, even though I understood that I had no right to expect any, or to challenge his decision. He opened a book, which began to speak.

'This is how I sent him to be born into an earthly body. Go to the earth, when you are born. I will bless you with a lot of wealth. You will use it to build many churches.'

The angel looked very upset at this point.

'See what he actually did,' the angel said. We went into yet another office, with a similar table to the one in the first room. On the table was another book, this time with the daily record of Ben's life written on the pages. On the current page the events were entered as they happened, minute-by-minute, hour-by-hour. Everything good or bad was there to read. Some pages were partly blank. It looked as though there had been writing on there but it was now erased. Every time he repented of wrong, the item was deleted so nothing could be read again or remembered. It was the duty of this angel to examine the quality of people's lives, whether they were making progress, or if they were getting worse. How awful if the decision was made that they were making no headway in improving their life, and heaven had decided to give him up. That's what the angel told me about Ben.

The record of Ben's life was horrible. I felt it gloomy and chilling. There were pages of criss-cross symbols and grave-looking bird skeletons. The feeling I got from looking at these pages was so awful I do not want to remember what I saw. The angel looked at me even more upset than before. He came close to me, and as he did so I felt that I was his companion in grief. 'I will give him a little longer to live if he repents and does what I have said. Nevertheless, he will have to come to you so that you may lay hands on him. If he does, I will forgive him. Now, go and tell him what I have said. I will come back to you a month before he is due to die and tell you more. GO!'

Those were powerful words. Two words are irresistible when God says them, the word 'go' and the word 'come'.

When he had finished saying that, I felt myself re-enter my body. It felt warm, but a little unpleasant. I woke Celia, who by this time was beginning to get used to my relationship with Jesus. She looked startled. I told her the story. She understood this was no joke. We discussed this and decided to hold a meeting to decide how to get this message across. Who was most likely to be listened to, not Celia or me, for sure? We met with Millie, Pastor John Kabuki and a few of Ben's family.

Ben was a wealthy executive based in Kampala city. He was the head of a well-known company exporting agricultural products. Spending his own money on building churches would challenge him in the area he would feel most confident and where his whole security lay. To him it was a noble custom to be a Christian, but only a custom. Was it wise to drain his whole life's sweat for such a thing?

Ben was also, like many men, touchy in the area of self-image. In company with many Africans of his age, sixty, people would feel demeaned if they based their actions on the advice of a mere woman and a bunch of his relatives who were known attendees of an unrecognized Christian sect. Who were Millie and Simeon to tell him how to run his life? Simeon he had known from a boy, and had as little regard for him as for a piece of paper blown into his back yard. For some reason Celia, for whom he had always had some respect, had married this man Simeon. Even the reports of some miracles associated with Simeon he could dismiss as hearsay.

Millie came back to us after speaking to her husband, who rejected our suggestion. He said he was a member of the Anglican Church that he was happy to pray for himself, and he wished us well, but would not be asking me to lay hands on him and pray. We continued to pray that Ben would change his mind. We even spent a whole night praying, with Millie's consent, for him in his house while he was away on a business safari.

About a month before the year was up, I had another visit from the angel who had spoken to me about Ben. This time I was standing on a kind of board in mid air. I sensed afterwards that the angel was really Jesus Christ Himself, but He appeared as an angel to me in this vision. He showed me a vision of Millie caring for her children on her own. She appeared to be arranging schools for them, at home and in another country.

She was also working out the details of how to provide for their daily needs and for hospital care. I saw next something looking like a gun and a telescope at the same time. As I looked through it, I saw the following scene. I watched Ben's everyday activities as if they were on a cinema screen. At the same time I heard,

> 'There is one month left. If he listens to me even now, I will give him longer to live. If he doesn't this is how he will die. Then you will know that I have spoken to you. Tell it before it happens so that when it comes to pass, they will remember that I have told you about it.'

Next, he looked at me like one of my O level teachers and said,

> 'This is how he will die. He will be standing at the front door of his house, with his son Charles beside him on the left. A gunman will rush up to him and will shoot Ben in the chest. Charles will be wearing khaki shorts and his short-sleeved white shirt will be splashed with blood. I will save Millie's life because she comes to worship Me and pray to Me daily in your church.'

I wondered why my church, of all places. I suppose it has something to do with the prayer that is offered in the place. I don't fully understand God's mind on this matter, but I do know that God hears prayer, and when He hears you praying in a particular place, He notices the place. A place is not important until God hears you praying there. I knew Ben would die unless he humbled himself and came to Namirembe Fellowship, a place he despised. The Holy Spirit had told me that our prayers would not be answered unless Ben made this decision. He would test the faith of many who considered themselves worthy by choosing a humbling situation such as this. This was why He would insist that Ben come to us and our prayer would be of no avail until he did.

We met in mid air with shared sadness, as we feared he would not listen. I felt increasingly close to my Friend. We were very aware of the duty, the assignment we were to carry out together, and a noble, eternal purpose to work out. We had a plan to put into action of enormous importance. I felt we shared a common responsibility binding us in everlasting friendship. We understood each other's needs and would spend a lifetime experiencing the long journey that lay ahead. I was so aware I am only a man. He is a King. How could a king be so humble? The glory of Jesus Christ is not in pomp, like that of earthly kings. His glory is clothed in simplicity, in humility, peace. It is not an artificial or contrived majesty. Jesus calls us to be His humble flock, His flock following humble shepherds, being herded by the humble King of kings. Jesus' followers should be a community of the simple and humble.

Still Ben would not listen to his wife, Millie. Millie shared her frustration and disappointment with me often as months reduced to weeks, weeks to days, days to hours and hours to minutes. This last month was a very tense one for all three of us, Millie, Celia and me. It also was hard on the prayer group. I had the burden of the Lord's message on my shoulders like a heavy pack of stones. What I feared most was that people would blame me for the message rather than Ben for his resistance. People usually prefer the simple option. They want an easy solution to any problem. One of the easiest solutions is to blame the person you like the least for the situation. I wished I could have kept my mouth shut. But how could I have kept quiet? It is a servant's duty to be obedient. I also feared that some people would think I had arranged the whole thing. They would suspect me of having planned it. I was not a criminal, far from it; I was only a tiny preacher. I remembered the passage,

'The natural man does not receive the things of the Spirit of God, for they are foolishness to him; nor can he know them, because they are spiritually discerned.' (1 Corinthians 2:14)

God's wisdom is different from ours. If we judge God's mind by men's standards, we can make a serious error. Most of our theories of psychology, science, sociology, politics, law and social standing do not take God into consideration at all. Those of us who take the revelation of God seriously are not considered as basing their actions on solid fact. All of us need that Man who I stood next to in mid air. The world places its trust in an imperfect temporal system, rejecting the promise of eternity. When exposed to the light of eternity, those things we rely on in this world, science, psychology, politics, law, wealth, knowledge and technology are profoundly diminished as a basis on which to depend for this life.

I woke up one morning afraid, after a bad dream. 'He is dead. What big fuss is there in rotting human flesh,' I heard in my sleep. Just then there was a loud knock on my bedroom door. It was Annette, house cleaner of Julia, Ben's sister. 'I have some bad news for you,' she said.

'Please don't mention it, I already know about it. Ben is dead isn't he?'

'Yes,' she replied. She too had been a member of our prayer group.

For two days the body lay in state in its expensive coffin as we paid our respects. Charles wore the same clothes until the funeral was over. As we had known it would be, there was a large bloodstain on his white short-sleeved shirt. His shorts were indeed army khaki. Millie had run to the basement when she heard the shots. The story was identical to the writing on the page I had seen a year earlier in my vision.

Whenever I remember this incident, the fear of the Lord comes back to me. After such a happening how could anyone deny God's existence? The whole family is deeply affected every time any of them remembers Ben. The prayer group at Namirembe was also deeply impacted by this event. That year of prayer is one of our most painful memories as we reflect on our strivings and deep desires, which went unmet in spite of all our loving concern. I do not know the state of Ben's soul at the time he died. Though many have asked me that question I do not know the answer. During the time of mourning some people asked me whether I thought Ben would be in heaven now. I reply, 'Yes, I think he could be. That depends on Jesus. Ben said he would pray for himself, I take that to mean he had some belief in Jesus, and possibly in private he had taken our message seriously.'

At the beginning of this chapter I said that it was our Lord who was on trial in the court of worldly wisdom. The accusation against Him is that talk of the devil is untrue. It is up to you to judge, after hearing about Ben, what you think about my contention that Satan tries to harden people's hearts against the saving truth. I say in defence of Jesus that what He says is true. His promises are valid. Heaven is a real place, and there actually is sentient life there.

No-one can escape the reality that Jesus is Lord and He holds the keys of heaven and hell. He has ultimate authority in all matters relating to this universe.

Chapter 7

Asking in Faith

I want to encourage you at this point. Be about to ask God for something. Several people were healed when they did just that after watching me give my testimony on television. I think I have given you enough evidence to ask God who is alive, listening to you, and will give you what you ask for. God is listening to you, whoever or wherever you are. It doesn't matter whether you have been given a poor prognosis from the doctor, or even if he is standing right at the end of your sick bed! It's not the doctor you should be afraid of; it's Almighty God who holds the keys of death. Don't be intimidated by your circumstances. Your request is valid; it's not too embarrassing for God to hear. Impossible situations are God's opportunity to show you how much He loves you by answering your prayer. He gave His life so you might have abundant life. If the situation looks unreasonable, it's His way of getting you out of trouble. When you are stuck, let Him make a way out for you. Let the storms of your life be calmed. Let there be a shift in wind direction. I write this with you especially in mind. I say this to you in Jesus' Name.

If you are reluctant to ask because you think it's not going to happen, I know someone who was in your shoes and got exactly what they expected! Don't delay because you have some doubt; just try it. Don't let your mind block your blessing. Jesus says, *'All things are possible to him who believes'*. I have seen many more miracles than there is room to write about in this book. They could easily fill another few books. My last twenty years have been full of surprises.

God's bank account

The main reason why Jesus came to earth was so that we might have life. Before God created the earth, He had no riches on earth. Through His creative word He became very rich indeed. God did not keep His wealth, a secret known only to Himself, He sent Jesus to declare it. We may have anything we want, if we ask Him.

> *'Whatever you ask the Father in My name He will give you.'*
> (John 16:23)

He continues by saying,

> *'Ask, and you will receive, that your joy may be full.'*
> (John 16:24)

Jesus, through whom all things were made, taught us that we too can use His Word to receive whatever we want from God, but we need to ask in His, Jesus', name. By faith in that name we can even relocate mountains from their present positions. We can dispossess diseases from their position in our bodies and have them go hissing into oblivion. Diseases removed, diminished, withered, forgotten, thoroughly dealt with and finished.

> *'Now in the morning, as they passed by, they saw the fig tree dried up from the roots. And Peter, remembering, said to Him, "Rabbi, look! The fig tree which You cursed has withered away." So Jesus answered and said to them, "Have faith in God. For assuredly, I say to you, whoever says to this mountain 'Be removed and be cast into the sea,' and does not doubt in his*

heart, but believes that those things he says will be done, he
will have whatever he says."'   (Mark 11:20–23)

In other words he shall be successful because of his faith. He
will see a breakthrough because of his faith. The darkness of
night that hangs over him will roll away in the dawn of a
miracle. It's madness to speak to a fig tree, but that is nothing
compared to the nonsense of speaking to things that are not,
as if they were. The voice that is loud enough or strong
enough to call something to exist out of nowhere is a force
to be reckoned with indeed. It sounds crazy to me to make
something out of nothing. Both the act of creation by speech
alone and to curse a fig tree are crazy things to do, but you had
better get used to the idea of doing some seemingly crazy
things and seeing them work when God is around.

You will not see the supernatural happening until you do
the inwardly disrupting, crazy thing. You have to take the
shocking, humanly speaking, irrational, immodest, radical,
unorthodox, irreligious thing of taking a step of faith. What
seems shocking to human eyes is spiritually beautiful to God.

'God said, "Let there be light"; and there was light. And God
saw the light, that it was good; and God divided the light from
the darkness.'   (Genesis 1:3–4)

God divided them like one would separate gold dust from
clay. God's Word has the power to make a difference in your
life. He can make out of the old man a new one. Just as night is
separate from day, He can change your situation into a totally
new one. The new, clear, luminous situation He called 'day',
the murky, impure, offensive and inconvenient remainder He
called 'night'. There will surely be a time when you need
something badly. Your confession 'In the Name of Jesus, let
there be . . . ' will make a huge difference in your life. You can
create your own unique paradise thorough faith in God.

God rests

Although Sabbath Day observance is no longer a mandatory requirement of our faith, resting one day a week still is an important practice, because it contains an important principle. When God finished making everything He was happy. He relaxed because He no longer had to create anything more. Anything else yet to be created would come from what was already there. So God rested, happy and relaxed. Adam needed a wife. In a short time, after a quick sleep, there she was, made out of one of his ribs. We wanted a long-range communication method between far away cities, and there it was, radio waves. Trees and plants, animal fluids and fungi yield medicinal substances. When humanity made a grave mistake, from a virgin birth the Son of God, Jesus Christ, came to save us from the disappointment of the Creator. When we didn't know how to obtain this salvation, out of our heart came faith. Because everything was made through Jesus, out of praying without doubt we have what we ask for.

Finished business

When Jesus paid the price, and said, *'It is finished!'* He gave us a *fait accompli*. Now, if you ask anything of God you are not doing anything wrong. I repeat, don't be embarrassed to ask anything of Him. Whatever you ask is a valid request. We already looked at John 14:12–14. Read it again. Jesus teaches us whatever we ask for in His name it is already ours. You have everything you need if you agree with Jesus and pray without any doubt. Say the word of faith and God will make it come to pass. If anyone tells you you are crazy answer, 'When you stop to think howcome you and I exist at all, then it's crazy. It is totally against the law of nature that we should be here talking. A voice called everything out of nothing, so something crazy must have happened at the beginning. So I am expecting what seems like empty space to hear me when I speak.' Someone has in effect said to you, 'I'm going to give you whatever you ask.' He's told you to do something that appears crazy. He's told you a fundamental change will occur in your life if you rely on Him. We can have what we need if we only ask in faith for it.

Hope's marriage

Hope and her husband, evangelist Joshua Kahwa, live in Plaistow, London, England with their daughter. I am sitting in Hounslow, at her friend Christine Nsubuga's home; in fact I was in Hounslow because of them. Christine works at Buckingham Palace. She visited Namirembe Christian Fellowship when she was in Uganda in 1987 along with her sister Janet Kashozi. They were interested to see if miracles really happen today. They came to see me in my office but wanted me to tell them a word from the Lord without telling me what they were asking God for. I told them that Janet was married, but Christine was not yet married. I told her she would go into town and there she would meet the man who would become her husband.

Joshua Kahwa also came to see me to ask if I could pray with him to help him find a wife. He wanted to get married but was finding it increasingly difficult to meet someone. I told him his wife was in town somewhere and he had better 'Go into town right away and find her.' He went into town to help a friend make the necessary purchases for the wedding of a friend of Hope. Hope met Joshua in a small shop in town. Remembering the short time he had just spent in my office gave him the courage to say the crazy thing. Full of joy they both came to see me. A few months later wedding bells rang out.

Some time later, it turned out on investigation that Hope's fallopian tubes were blocked. Surgery would not help her, she would be unable to have children. Joshua came to see me in some distress, and was even more upset by my reaction. I slapped him cheerfully on the back and told him not to worry, just go and buy some nappies because they were going to need them, since his wife was going to conceive. Joshua did as I told him, and in that same month Hope fell pregnant. Patience, their daughter, is now eight years old. Hope has also had investigations in England. The consultant at Newham Hospital confirmed the state of her tubes is such that she can never conceive. But I already have one daughter, she told the astonished man. 'That was surely a miracle,' he said.

Both Hope and Joshua had heard of the miracles happening today in Uganda before they came to Namirembe Christian Fellowship. Joshua was born in Fort Portal about two hundred miles away from Kampala, where he heard the story I am about to tell you. Near Lake Kagadi lived a lady who had been unhappily married to a heavy drinker for over ten years. She had come to one of our associated fellowships to help her cope with the stress of this relationship. In 1985 she accepted Jesus as her Lord and Saviour. However, there was no change in the state of her marriage. Her husband was upset that she had joined what he called 'Kayiwa's religion'. He planned to set her aside on the grounds of her 'outlandish religion'. He meant this as a calculated insult; we believers do not consider followers of Jesus religious, but in relationship with Him, not the followers of a man.

One day he gave her some money to keep for him. She decided to put it under her pillow. He took the money without telling her and lost it while he was out fishing on Lake Kagadi. When he returned home he was very angry with his wife and demanded the money. She had no idea how it had disappeared from where she had put it. Her husband, by now inebriated and furious, started swearing, hitting her and kicking her viciously. Her told her he would kick her out of the house unless she produced the money within four days. At her wits end she travelled all the way to Namirembe Christian Fellowship to see me. When she entered the counselling room, she was advised to go home and believe that Jesus would bring the lost money back to her. She had faith and went back home.

Lake Kagadi is a favourite spot for recreation. Many people go there to fish and enjoy the beautiful beaches. The husband, a teacher, probably lost the money when he went for a swim. The purse must have fallen out of his pocket and dropped to the bottom of the lake. The lady decided to pray earnestly about the lost money, asking Jesus who alone knew the answer to her problem. He alone could vindicate her. He alone would be the judge of who was right. As she was praying like this, she heard a bicycle bell. It was a fisherman selling his catch. She chose a fat Nile perch, her favourite food, for tea. When she opened the fish up before cooking it, what do you think she found? You guessed, it was the missing purse, complete with the money. She screamed out 'I don't believe it!'

When the cruel husband returned drunk and noisy he bumped his head on the doorway and swore more than usual. But he stopped real quick when he saw the purse in her hand. 'Where did you get that from?!' 'From the fish,' his wife replied.

He dropped to his knees as if hit by a bullet. 'My God, my God, You are God! Forgive me, my God.'

His wife could not quite understand. He was no longer swearing. He gave his heart to Jesus there and then, and told his astonished wife the full story. They later came all the way to Namirembe Christian Fellowship to tell the whole church. What joy! You can imagine the praise that night was deafening.

Rhoda's miracle

Rhoda's husband was poor and could not provide shoes for his pregnant wife when she needed to go to hospital. I first set eyes on Rhoda as she walked past on her way to the hospital. It was in 1981 when the country was still in its state of anarchy and the noise of gunshots was in the air. She looked very pregnant indeed. She wore an old pair of bedroom slippers as she travelled to the hospital a few metres away from where we held our prayer meetings. Her dress was so tight it looked as though it would squeeze the suffocating baby out of her like toothpaste. Her red eyes and shaggy hair announced the poverty of her family. She ran the gamut of the lousy conversation of the soldiers who not infrequently would rape the women and rip the babies from their bellies while they were in hospital. Despair filled our hearts when those crim-inals occupied State House. No-one had the power to protect her. Everyone was wrapped up in his or her own struggle to survive. Millions of richer people left the country, preferring to live in exile.

She had no idea anyone cared for her when I called out. 'Hello there.' Neither of us had seen the other before, but she stopped. I introduced myself and advised her not to continue her journey but to stop with us and pray until I said it was safe. She was taking an enormous risk, but she did stop. For whatever reason she decided she was not going home and sent word to her family she was going to stay with us. She then told me of her extreme financial hardship. I replied that I didn't have any more money than she, which she could see for herself was true. 'I have nothing to offer but the promises of God,' I told her.

Four days later I told her it was safe to go, but she expected me to give her some money. When I didn't give her any, she had difficulty understanding me. She didn't realise the Bible could be believed in a practical way. As far as she was concerned one would read the Bible to practise belief in God, but to trust it for provision was another dimension. Yes, I was the sort of person you could talk to, but I had nothing to offer her. My job is to reveal the fact that Jesus can be relied on in a very practical way. By saying this I was not trying to get out of giving to Rhoda. Jesus was teaching us all that He really is her shepherd and will cover her needs in a practical way. Rhoda walked out of the yard, and just at that moment a flying sack stopped her progress! A Peugeot 404 thumped over a pothole, the boot opened and out dropped the sack.

It was full of nappies, baby clothes, maternity dresses and clothes suitable for after a birth including shoes, which were just the right size for Rhoda. We kept the sack for a week and advertised on the lost and found announcements on the radio that we had it, but no-one came to claim it, so we gave it to Rhoda. The clothes were all for a baby girl, so she had advance warning of the sex of her unborn child.

Chapter 8

Overcoming Fear

Modern civilisation is like ripe fruit, a big, yellow, perishable fruit at the peak of readiness to be eaten, a juicy pear or papaya. When you pick it fresh it is delicious. After a while it starts to rot from the inside. Maggots may even grow in the core, but in appearance it still looks good to eat. The outward appearance of good manners, religious observance and the like is maintained in today's society, but family relationships and society's coherence are seriously eroded. In our homes we see rudeness, cursing and swearing, badly behaved children and many kinds of sexual immorality including homosexuality, but still function as respectable citizens at work. We live in what some have called a post-Christian culture. Christian values are no longer considered relevant in a post-modern society. What feels right, is right. Ours is a sex, party and rock and roll life style. I regard this relativistic moral climate as a deception, an excuse for debauchery, everyone following a hedonistic, selfish, immoral path; indeed I will go so far as to call it a perverted mindset. God has called us to live pure and holy lives. God knows we should do what He expects or perish. Tragically many famous celebrities have no time for God. Glossy magazines parade the sexual exploits and drunken brawls of the famous. A recent television programme trailer asked the question 'Are celebrities good role models?' Most of the time it is assumed their lifestyles are to be envied and copied without question. Musicians, boxers, soccer players, dancers, politicians, businessmen even some doctors have thousands of followers. Such luminaries are almost worshipped. We follow their siren songs of sexual immorality, witchcraft and occult practices. Multitudes of worshippers waving myrtle and palm fronds, join the bandwagon echoing in chorus transcending racial and national boundaries.

It is extremely difficult in these times for a preacher to have much effect in stemming this tide of misplaced worship. We compete with the best presentation television can offer, the most professional PR machines, all subtly undermining traditional values by means of seductive melodies, addictive internet programmes and the disappointment with people's expectations of God. Without the power of God it is impossible for pastors to resist being dragged into the same snare as our congregations.

It is not good enough for us as Christians to console ourselves with the second coming of the Lord, when many have not met Him for the first time. It is sheer foolishness to speculate on dates when the world around us is falling apart for lack of clear guidance. The very Church that Jesus left in trust has fallen from the demonstration of power in the Holy Ghost to petty bickering over theology.

Sins such as greed, gluttony, love of money, covetousness and pride are obvious to many would be worshippers in Spirit and Truth. Even some preachers have become tired and no longer take the trouble to accurately quote Bible references. They give boring repeats of talks prepared long ago, instead of seeking the Lord for a *rhema* word that will inspire, edify and motivate the flock. This disinterest makes fertile ground for Satan to misrepresent and discourage the faithful. Even worse, it allows perverted appetites their head. The ground will quake, church spires will collapse and the saints of stone will fall to the ground in shame on the Day of His Return! I am aware every time I pray and see a miracle that I serve Jesus who said, *'I am coming soon'*. He wants the whole world to know He is the greatest power in heaven and earth.

It's now twenty-one years since He first gave me this message. I believe that there is a probationary period of time set in heaven to see what each person will do with this information, a time set within which they have the opportunity to decide to follow the Lord, a time of mercy during which God waits to see what man's free will make of His invitation to follow Him. There will come a time when God's Spirit will no longer struggle with man's conscience. When that time is up, there will no longer be space for a change of heart, no power left by which sinners will be saved. Miracles are a sign of God's appeal of love to the world. They are Christ's plea of love and mercy, His tears of anticipation of the outcome. They are warnings and reproofs which man has the free will to meet with blind scorn and cruel rebuffs.

I am very concerned about the condoning of homosexual acts by the Church. I have even heard it declared from the pulpit, 'Beloved, due to human error, maybe some of our brethren here are trapped in a male body when they were supposed to be female. We should pray for them, understand them and encourage them to make their own choices as intelligent children of our loving God.' Someone in the crowd is heard to say, 'Amen!' What a defeated church. If Jesus corrected His own disciples after they had been unsuccessful at an attempted deliverance, by pointing out they needed faith as a grain of mustard seed, which they could get by prayer and fasting (Matthew 17:20–21), what would He make of those who condone sin and do not practise these disciplines, who claim to be His disciples today?

There are necessary limits to freedom if we wish to live holy lives. Paul tells Timothy,

> '*Guard what was committed to your trust, avoiding the profane and idle babblings and contradictions of what is falsely called knowledge – by professing it some have strayed concerning the faith.*'   (1 Timothy 6:20–21)

I think we would all agree that sexual exploitation is unacceptable behaviour for Christians. It is particularly unacceptable to say, 'my feelings say it is OK', or worse, 'they asked me to do so', when an adult takes sexual pleasure from a child. To offer their nature as justification for men seducing boys, and to campaign for greater legality for this practice is an affront to biblical teaching. The marriage bed should be undefiled (Hebrews 13:4). The devil has tried to use the notion of nature to confuse the intellectual, politician, lawyer, philosopher and preacher. Nature has become not just a stumbling block for the individual; it is fast becoming a veritable mountain of deception. What can we do? We can speak to this mountain and cast the mountain away.

The effect of such corruption in our inner man is in several layers. Our heart is defiled, our hope weakened, our intellect blunted, our conscience perverted, our flesh can manifest illness and our emotions become agonised. We career into a nightmarish pit of despair. We end up deceiving ourselves spiritually. In marriage godly behaviour should be demonstrated in the following way. Small arguments should be resolved in a spirit of submission, by apology for wrong done, repentance and reconciliation. Instead we see a vicious circle of disagreement escalating to argument, emotional and physical abuse, ending in breakdown of the partnership and filing for divorce. Sexual infidelity can be a symptom or a cause of this breakdown. Ultimately the AIDS epidemic is the latest plague to affect humanity from the combination of bestiality, homosexuality and heterosexual infidelity.

Our whole social structure in Africa is under threat in the present age. Men's minds are preoccupied with discrimination against their fellow men. People maliciously plan murder, theft, embezzlement and misappropriation of state funds, war, lies and oppression. Racial discrimination, especially in the job market, is rife, bad-mouthing those who are financially more successful, cheating the poor, weak, ill, orphans and widows. Some politicians will not eschew any underhand means to secure their election. They draw the gullible with empty promises and attract many disadvantaged to vote for them, who do not realise their mistake until it is too late to get rid of them. They especially appeal to the less moral sectors of society, which ends up being very bad for all of us, who have to try and live with the shame of the destiny they have helped shape. The root of injustice lies in the heart. When we refuse to obey the urgings in our God-given consciences, we bring this desperate state on ourselves and become prey to Satan.

One major entrance for this vicious cycle is the emotion of fear. What can we do about fear? When some difficult problems occur, we say, 'I can't cope any more.' Living under fear affects all our relationships. It undermines our confidence, and those who live timidly are robbed of their credibility by the reaction of others. 'If he is so anxious, he must have doubts about this', is the instinctive reaction created in others. Fear releases the fight or flight hormone, adrenaline, into our blood stream. Fear is such an unpleasant emotion; we may resort to any means to escape its clutches. Alcohol, drugs and other addictive behaviour may be one way of dealing with a fearful approach to life. 'I'm ready to resign, I'll just have time out and have a smoke, or a drink on the way home.'

I have observed at least one soldier find consolation in sex with a prostitute or unwilling rape victim. Another soldier goes mad and fires around him wildly in panic. A housewife ends up shouting and cursing at every living soul in her house. I have seen bus drivers totally ignore red traffic lights, surgeons lose instruments inside patients because of chronic anxiety and dictators declare states of emergency unnecessarily, all from fear. Everything is at sixes and sevens when fear rules our planet.

Jesus came to our planet to reverse this insidious decay. Through Him the world should have hope. Through Him an anticipation of revival should arise instead of fear. God loved the world so much that fear should be vanquished through dependency on Jesus. No man had such a fearless heart as Jesus. No-one else in history had such a heart as He. There was nothing He encountered that caused Him to fear; not storms at sea, rioting crowds, diseases of all sorts or unscrupulous politicians, no-one made Him react out of fear in all these examples. Not even His own destiny, to die for the sins of the world, caused Him anxiety. Jesus faced it all with joy as the book of Hebrews tells us,

> '... *for the joy that was set before Him endured the cross, despising the shame ...*' (Hebrews 12:2)

Trust in Jesus is the answer to a fearful mindset.

> '*Perfect love casts out all fear.*' (1 John 4:18)

We can be assured by the presence of Jesus, His demonstration of love in His death and resurrection, that we too can be victorious over fear. We are then free to fulfil our command to multiply and subdue the whole earth. We were not born to have dust and ashes overwhelm us, to spread a blanket over us to hide our efforts from sight, but rather that we should stamp our mark resolutely, powerfully, marching around the globe declaring the praises of our Redeemer. We plant our feet, like a footballer placing the ball before the decisive penalty goal ready for victory, to say, 'In the Name of Jesus, I speak out, "World, today I am master, you are servant, I subdue you, you are given to me to control. Tempests or earthquakes, I shall not move, you must obey!"'

When we trust Jesus our hearts are filled with His love and we find God deals with the anguish of suffering, replacing our fear of the future with His comfort. God associates Himself deeply with our suffering, weeping with us when we weep and sighing with us when we sigh. He ministers to the deepest level of our personality. Let's look at a few examples from the Bible and take comfort from remembering the One who weeps and sighs with us.

Remember the story of Lazarus we looked at earlier? I find the episode where Mary came rushing to Jesus weeping to tell Him of the death of her brother one of the most comforting passages in the Bible.

> *'Then, when Mary came where Jesus was, and saw Him, she fell down at His feet, saying to Him, "Lord, if You had been here, my brother would not have died." Therefore when Jesus saw her weeping, and the Jews who came with her weeping, He groaned in the spirit and was troubled. And He said to them, "Where have you laid him?" They said to Him, "Lord, come and see." Jesus wept. Then the Jews said, "See how He loved him!" ... Then Jesus, again groaning in Himself, came to the tomb.'*   (John 11:32–36, 38)

The identification of Jesus with the grief of His friends is clearly seen. Who doesn't need to see Jesus' tears when they are going through trouble? The unbelieving Jews were also able to observe Jesus' love by the emotion He clearly showed.

Then, as if brandishing the rod of authority against the power of death, the weeping Jesus said, *'Take away the stone.'* And after a short delay, *'Lazarus, come forth!'* The mourners were unable to get beyond the evidence of their own eyes. Martha even says to Him, *'Lord, by this time there is a stench.'* For a moment they did not see Jesus as the God who does the impossible, only the experience of natural consequences. They did not dare to trust Jesus as the resurrection. But when they started to believe, they took the stone away.

I see Jesus displaying the quality of empathy in abundance here. He wept and sighed with Mary. He conveyed to all around His sharing of her inner ordeal. Martha interpreted Jesus' promise of resurrection to be a comforting thought for the distant future. She was not expecting a literal fulfilment in the immediate future. She felt honoured to have His presence with her in her hour of grief; she felt soothed by His words *'Your brother will rise again'* (John 11:23). I get a similar sense when I read the story of the Good Samaritan. Here was a wounded traveller honoured by the attention of a wealthy merchant on his way to Jericho. The first thing to remember when you are suffering is that you have a Caring Friend.

Today I am meeting Tom Martin, who made the trip from Ireland specially to see me after reading about some of the miracles God has done for us at Namirembe Christian Fellowship. We discuss the kind heart of Mother Teresa, who would comfort sick people dying in her arms. It has particular relevance as we are staying in the home of Christine Nsubuga who works in a Nursing Home in Hounslow. We talk about the simple demeanour of Jesus, how His tears of sympathy did not diminish His power in any way.

Jesus first identified with the sufferer and then found a solution suitable for the situation. With Adam He identified Adam's loneliness, his boredom and lack of purpose without a suitable partner. He then administered heavenly anaesthetic, putting Adam to sleep. Adam was not required to exercise faith at that time. Because it was before the fall, he was in the full presence of the Lord all the time, but things were different for Mary and Martha. Faith was necessary for the miracle. First Jesus had to create an atmosphere conducive to faith, by dealing with fear. Fear disturbs faith. In a bad environment fear not faith can get the upper hand. Mother Teresa, by her care, created a loving environment so that it was easier for the sick person to pray. With the right kind of encouragement, the patient may be ready at the feet of Jesus, at the place to receive a miracle.

Jesus' tears proved how deep His love for His friend Lazarus was. Jesus genuinely missed His friend, and wept. This comforted Mary, encouraged her and enabled her belief to come into use. So she believed in a miracle. The miracle of Lazarus' resurrection then happened. If a person is your friend, you believe in him. Jesus is available; He is simple, personable, approachable, and able to empathise perfectly with your suffering.

When we are at the lowest point emotionally, we weep. The way to express the despair in our soul is to weep. We all have times when we desperately need a shoulder to cry on. It is a great help when we have a friend to confide in. Some people may try to make us feel better by saying such things as, 'It happens to everyone', or 'Many people have gone through worse than you have to deal with.' They dismiss your suffering as an attitude problem. You may even agree with them that a change of attitude on your part would be a solution to the problem, but until you see your special friend it doesn't make you feel any better. What you need is the evidence of a caring heart. And you need a particular person to demonstrate this care. Mary and Martha were waiting for their special Friend who would listen with genuine concern for them. Martha's faith could reach to knowing that Jesus' presence would have prevented Lazarus' death. But Jesus had not been there to prevent it and now she needed so much to talk to Him. She knew her aching heart would be calmed when she shared her trouble with Jesus.

Was there ever a time when you were going through a particularly bad time and you felt God entering your bitterest situation and sharing its pain? Do you remember Jesus empathising deeply with you at your lowest moment and saying, *'I will be with you.' 'I will never leave you, or forsake you.' As I was with Moses, so I will be with you.'* Did you notice Him weeping when someone mistreated you, when you failed those exams or failed to win that sports event or that election? Mary was honoured that such an important person as the rabbi Jesus should come to see her in her grief. Tears ran down His face so all the onlookers exclaimed, 'See how He loved him.'

Pause for a minute and think about this, teardrops running down the face of the Son of God. The love that releases tears is deep love indeed. It operates beyond the confines of modesty when we allow our face to publicly express our emotion in tears.

I know God empathises with us in our deepest hour of need. I was involved in defending myself in court some time ago. What made the situation particularly unpleasant was that the prosecution case was based on the lies a former friend of mine was spreading about me. Someone who I had trusted and regarded as a special friend turned against me and started saying all sorts of things that were reported in the newspapers. He had taken to writing articles, which he duplicated and circulated widely, both in Uganda and abroad. One day one of the Calvary Choir members found me sobbing, tears running freely down my cheeks, I was taking it so hard. I was deeply embarrassed to be found showing such weakness and tried to cover it up, hastily steeling myself to act as if I was not distressed on my own account. I forced a smile at her and spoke to her. I didn't want any human being to witness me crying. I longed for a particular Heart to answer that cry. Those teardrops expressed the deepest feelings of my soul. They were prayer in liquid form.

I could not rely on human sympathy at that time. Many people had already started to believe what they were reading. I was angry and afraid. I was not in need of human solutions; this situation needed divine intervention. It needed God.

My tears represented the inexpressible groaning of my spirit to my Lord. Through these experiences I learned the reality of the Holy Spirit, the Comforter. Jesus refers to the Holy Spirit with this title in John 14:26 and 16:7 (AV). At this time of anger, fear and threat I needed to feel the comfort of the One who had adopted me as His son. It's so good to know the Holy Spirit wants us to turn our tear-streaked face to the Father crying to Him, 'Abba, Abba'.

> *'For you did not receive the spirit of bondage again to fear, but*
> *you received the Spirit of adoption by whom we cry out, "Abba,*
> *Father."'*   (Romans 8:15)

When we pray in this manner, it is the same Spirit who once cried in Gethsemane to the Father, crying within us. In Gethsemane Jesus was *'exceedingly sorrowful, even to death'* we read in Mark 14:34. He walked a few paces away from His disciples and *'fell on the ground, and prayed that if it were possible, the hour might pass from Him. And He said, "Abba, Father, all things are possible for You. Take this cup away from Me; nevertheless, not what I will, but what You will"* (Mark 14:35b–36). Jesus, who wept at Lazarus' grave, was weeping here drops of blood. The cup has never been taken away. The same Jesus, who wept there, has more friends today than in those days to visit and to weep with. If you will believe His presence will make the difference in your life, you will experience the comfort of His tears. When I weep at the sight of someone's distress, whose are the tears on my face?

For a very good reason the cup was never taken from Jesus. When I wept, the cup that was mine was taken from me, judgement was pronounced in my favour and the cup was given to Him. On this first occasion when my former friend was pursuing me in court, this revelation comforted me. The God of the Bible is personal.

> *'And because you are sons, God has sent forth the Spirit of His*
> *Son into your hearts, crying out, "Abba, Father!"'*
> (Galatians 4:6)

I can picture Him with tears in His eyes as He sits with Mary and Martha crying, 'Abba, Father'. All at once the court found in my favour. I forgave my friend and later we were reconciled.

The deepest hurt a pastor can experience is that the people he has led into freedom in Christ turn against him and start causing divisions in the church fellowship he has laboured so dedicatedly to nurture. In spite of the many miracles I have witnessed, my story is also one of severe strains, hostile schisms and struggles within Namirembe Christian Fellowship, breaking out at times into undignified public scenes. Sometimes the cuts went so deep it was like potato chips in hot oil. Everyone wanted to be honoured. Everyone was covetous for political power. I had to endure the most scathing criticism that hell could inspire from ambitious competitors who set up rival churches. New churches were springing up all over the country. I was denounced as a false prophet from new and old pulpits.

'Don't go near that false prophet Simeon who screams daily at the road junction near the mango tree on the highway between the two towns of Nakulabye and Mengo.'

Warnings issued from centuries old pulpits reverberated throughout the country. Prayer warriors were even fasting, appealing to God for my death! At Christmas and Easter broadcasts on radio and television issued warnings about me. From churches, mosques, witchdoctors and shrines I heard the angry chorus, 'Do not go there, lest you be infected by his pernicious doctrines and demons. Demons will swarm over you like bees and will bite the hell out of you. You will get cancer, curses, and all manner of diseases. To crown it all, he has no neat, well-built buildings there. He would have you die in his type of poverty.'

I had to turn to Jesus to feel His tears at my unjust vilification. All these human obstacles were turned into God's stepping-stones because Jesus was observing all the events, witnessing everything. When Jesus is in the house, it turns the situation around.

> '*And again He entered Capernaum after some days, and it was heard that He was in the house. Immediately many gathered together, so that there was no longer room to receive them.*'
>
> (Mark 2:1–2)

My challenges made me more determined to work harder to demonstrate my calling. It was like the time when Robert Saidi had doubted my encounter with Jesus that first time, I was motivated into a deeper desire for miracles. Amazingly my efforts were blessed with increasing numbers of new believers until it became a nation-wide revival. People the length and breadth of Uganda were singing that Jesus is the greatest power in heaven and earth. Out of this hive of activity have emerged many preachers who are now roaming far beyond Uganda with their message.

I love the words of John Newton's famous hymn:

> Amazing grace! How sweet the sound
> that saved a wretch like me.
> I once was lost, but now am found;
> was blind but now I see.
>
> Through many dangers, toils and snares
> I have already come.
> 'Tis grace that brought me safe thus far,
> and grace will lead me on.

Chapter 9

Protected by God

I had been preaching for several years with disapproval from the older Christian churches. I felt under a dark grey cloud as I maintained my lonely stand. I felt the establishment's laughter when I declared boldly that miracles were happening in the name of Jesus to people in the local community. They were still convinced that I did not know what I was talking about. In spite of all this new members were added to us daily.

Among these was a man called Joachim Kategaya who forced his way onto the platform interrupting the whole service. His voice was feeble and wavering due to a long-standing illness the nature of which he did not reveal. He asked for prayer for healing and also help in finding accommodation, as he was also homeless. We took him into our home and prayed for him regularly. By the time a month was over he was looking perfectly healthy, not a trace of weakness at all, and he was well enough to return to work.

Joachim owned two cars. In appreciation of his return to health he decided to give me one of the cars, a Fiat. This would help me in my ministry to the sick, as I would travel all over the country, visiting people who asked for my help. He even put this in writing to me. A couple of months later I was to get a nasty shock. I was due to preach at the Lunch Hour Fellowship in Kampala City. I was quite accustomed to seeing large crowds of people assembled outside waiting for the opportunity to be prayed for. But this day the crowd was different. Angry shouts of 'Thief! Thief!' rang in my ears. It was like a swarm of locusts waiting to devour me. Some even pelted me with stones. I was very glad there were some police in the crowd also waiting for me as the situation could have easily escalated way out of control very quickly. I could have been torn limb from limb by the vultures before help could arrive if they hadn't been on the spot at that precise moment. This was still in the anarchic days when a thief would have been dealt with by mob rule. 'Red hot mob justice' we called it. Plastic material would be tied round his body and petrol poured over him, then set alight. In no time he would be rendered into ash.

I had better pray.

Two burly policemen, eyes so hot with anger that blood stained tears escaped, flanked me. Roughly they ordered me down to the Central Police Station. These men were almost coughing fire and brimstone, they were so hostile. The charge they explained to me was of using 'the crafty manoeuvre of religious indoctrination' to obtain a car. Under a 'cocoon of religion' was 'hiding a most wanted criminal'. Today I could hide no longer.' Luckily for me, we had gone through all the necessary documentation to transfer ownership of the vehicle and Joachim was soon at the Central Police Station with the paperwork. I was quite prepared to hand the car back again, but Joachim was made of sterner stuff and insisted as a matter of principle on setting the record straight in spite of the group of outraged family surrounding him. When a small crowd containing his father, wife, several uncles, cousins and other strange looking characters gathered it made him angry and he stiffly refused more stubbornly to give in to them.

After a brief interview with 'prisoner Simeon', the charge was promptly dismissed. At this the crowd, bar one, Joachim's Cousin Sam, melted away. Sam threatened to maintain the accusation until he had put me under the sole of his foot. Sam's parting shot was to declare he would hire either a hit man or a witchdoctor to finish me off. 'Who do you think you are, you man, whatever people call you?' I advised him to make it up with his cousin and come to a joint decision about the car. I would abide by whatever decision they came to. I did not want to be party to exacerbating a family dissention. I told him I was not prepared to fight anyone over the possession of a car.

'What a fool you are,' replied Sam. 'How dare you get involved?' Who do you think you are? I am not talking to that sick man.'

'I suppose I am nobody. All I can say is that I am a preacher. I know you can kill me if God permits it, you really can. If Jesus wants to protect me, He will.' was my reply.

'Who is your God?' he sneered.

An elderly lady tried to reason with him. 'I'm sure he will hand the car back to your cousin if that is what you want,' she said.

But by this time Joachim was adamant. 'My blood is really up,' he said. 'By the way why are you so concerned for me? Who are you? Are you my relative? How come I do not know you? You are just a thief trying to confuse the mind of my old father and relatives!' 'Leave me alone! I am an adult,' continued Sam.

The police advised me to go to court if I wanted to take things further, having witnessed his death threat. It was a tough decision. This was back in 1985, when police could easily be bribed and a man's life could easily be snuffed out in this manner. 'Smoked away' was our term. I told Celia and the Calvary Cross Choir members, the people I most valued as confidants and prayer warriors. They advised me to go into hiding.

That night Joachim came to tell me the police were once again looking for me. This time, however it was to apologise for what had happened. Joachim told me that after I had left Sam started to walk down the road. He was still shouting angrily when a car speeded by killing him instantly. The same police who had watched everything now carried him to the hospital. They were surprised to find that in fact Sam was not related in any way to Joachim. He was in fact someone a disgruntled relative of Joachim had hired. This relative belonged to a religious sect opposed to the gospel, which Joachim had formerly belonged to. They suspected Sam of having been involved with a popular form of blackmail whereby celebrities and people with money were accused falsely with court action. They threatened exposure of their embarrassing, but false, accusations to the papers. This would result in large out of court settlements in order to avoid the media publicity. Sometimes they would even get so bold as to threaten to kill them and claimed they were working with police knowledge and approval. Some of the police hierarchy and senior Army officers were even sometimes corrupt enough at that time to actually be involved in these protection rackets, demanding money on a daily basis. We were told that the angry crowd had been hired to shout at me.

How amazing is this deliverance, going completely against the tide of corruption that was rife in those days. I love to stroll down memory lane, giving Jesus the glory for keeping me safe through that troubled period of Uganda's history. I sing praise to the great name of Almighty God, the greatest Power in earth and heaven. I think often about victory situations such as these. I love to tell Jesus,

> *'Yea, though I walk through the valley of*
> *   the shadow of death,*
> *I will fear no evil;*
> *For You are with me;*
> *Your rod and Your staff they comfort me.'*   (Psalm 23:4)

The shepherd's staff

In ancient Israel a shepherd would carry a wooden stick, a staff or crook, to help him in his work. Whenever a special event happened in his life, he would record it by engraving his staff. That way he would indelibly fix the event in his mind. As he went about his business he would feel the marks engraved into the wood and take courage from his previous victories. Hope would rise as his hands felt the record of previous achievements. David had a particularly richly carved staff. It was like a mosaic testifying of God's ever-present love, grace, power and faithfulness. His crook, like a diary, bore a statement of the appreciation to God. I can imagine him sitting down sometimes with his eyes closed, deliberately feeling the marks and reminding himself of the various expressions of God's love to him that the experiences taught him. David caressed the memories one by one. The lion that had threatened the whole livelihood of the family as it bore down on the youngest member of the family, not yet strong enough to do man's work, so sent to talk to the sheep. The bear he had later torn to pieces with his bare hands. These episodes had caused him to overcome his fear of the wild beasts, his enemies. By the power of God he wrote,

> 'Yea, though I walk through the valley of
>   the shadow of death,
> I will fear no evil;
> For You are with me;
> Your rod and Your staff they comfort me.
> You prepare a table before me in the presence
>   of my enemies.'
> (Psalm 23:4–5)

David was able to see that the same care he had for his family flocks was the same as God has for His people. *'The LORD is my shepherd'* (Psalm 23:1). The Lord, as shepherd, has comforting experiences for all believers. This has happened from time immemorial. We can comfortably take refuge in Him and be safe.

> *'God is our refuge and strength,*
> *A very present help in trouble.*
> *Therefore we will not fear,*
> *Even though the earth be removed,*
> *And though the mountains be carried into the*
>   *midst of the sea;*
> *Though its waters roar and be troubled,*
> *Though the mountains shake with its swelling . . .*
> *The LORD of hosts is with us;*
> *The God of Jacob is our refuge.'*   (Psalm 46:1–3, 7)

The Bible seems to me like a great big shepherd's staff, engraved with sacred experiences of God's multiple victories achieved for His people over Satan. It is important to record our victories and make a diary of the ground we have covered in our walk with God. When our hand caresses the staff we are emboldened to face the future.

When David remembered his past, he was ready to face Goliath. He argued,

> *'Who is this uncircumcised Philistine, that he should defy the armies of the living God? . . . The LORD, who delivered me from the paw of the lion and from the paw of the bear, He will deliver me from the hand of this Philistine.'*
>
> (1 Samuel 17:26b, 37)

So Saul gave his blessing to David's challenge. David, of course, as we are familiar with the end of the story, goes on to defeat the mighty Goliath who had terrified the cream of the Israelite fighters.

After my ordeal with the crowd and the law, Joachim came

to me with words of comfort. My wife, family and choir had advised me to stop preaching and go into hiding, but he came telling me that it was fine to continue as the policeman who had formerly arrested me, and who we suspected was part of a trap, was looking for me to apologise for my wrongful arrest. His encouragement emboldens me to trust the Lord through great dangers, trials and snares.

The story of Mary, Joseph and Jesus' return to Galilee from Egypt after the death of Herod is another Bible story that I turn to in moments of crisis. Children had been massacred on a vast scale after the indiscriminate decree designed to kill the newborn King Jesus Christ. An angel warned Joseph to take his family to Egypt urgently. Eventually Herod died and it was safe for the family to return to Galilee.

> *'Now when Herod was dead, behold, an angel of the Lord appeared in a dream to Joseph in Egypt, saying, "Arise, take the young Child and His mother, and go to the land of Israel, for those who sought the young Child's life are dead." '*
>
> (Matthew 2:19–20)

It reminds me of the fate of Sam when I read this account. His was not the only threat I received. Someone else promised worse.

Sixty-year-old Julia came to Namirembe Christian Fellowship in 1980 asking for prayer. Later she became a valued member of the ministry team. She had a daughter called Celia. Celia was studying in Vichy, France for a diploma in the French language. I fell in love with her on 18th April and we were married on May 16th 1981, a month later. It was only for the love of God that we survived. We should by rights be lying in state on the 18th May and be buried on 19th. Let me explain.

On the day of our wedding gunmen intercepted a pickup truck containing all our presents before it reached our house.

The vehicle and the presents were never seen again. Next, the photographer hired to take the wedding shots fraudulently had no film in his camera so we have no record of the day. In spite of several letters foretelling an unhappy end to our precipitate marriage, the Reverend Canon Cyprian Kibuka invited us to celebrate with a dinner party at his home. Dinner was served at 8 p.m. Celia and I sat with the Canon and Kate his wife, ready to eat the magnificent meal they had prepared. Sweet instrumental music wound itself around every corner of the room from the concealed record player. Our spirits were joyful in that cheerful atmosphere and we expected to live happily ever after. Everything seemed to say 'Hello there!' The onions smelt delicious in the exquisite china dishes, used only for special feasts. The electric light burned brightly. Things couldn't have appeared rosier.

All of a sudden I had an urgent warning in my spirit. 'Get down on the floor, now!' I commanded. We all flung ourselves flat on the floor at just the same moment that a hail of gunshots sprayed across the dinner table. Not even a cock-roach could have stayed asleep for five miles around. Celia started screaming as she frantically put her hands to her head. 'Thimeon, Theemeon, I think I've been shot!' She tried to burrow under me for comfort. If she could have, she would have struggled right inside my body. All of us were in the same position, tossed around the room like mushrooms in hot butter as glass shattered all around us, into our hair and spoiling all the sumptuous food. It took us some time to pick up the spent shells and examine ourselves. Amazingly not one of us was harmed, although it took me some time to convince Celia that she had not really suffered any injury, and she took a while before she was able to stop crying. We picked up the shells and discovered that if we had been a moment later Julia would certainly have been hit in the head, and Celia and I would have been pinned together at the chest with the same bullet.

The smell of onion had been obliterated by the smell of gunpowder. The hit-man was without doubt after us and was firing at very close range. I don't know how he could have missed if God had not given us that time to take action. We could not understand the motive for the attack. It could have had something to do with the beautiful girl I had married, or someone who envied the large following we had gathered at the Namirembe Christian Fellowship. Whatever, I'm of the opinion that someone was angry, jealous, ambitious or afraid of the Fellowship or us. Praise God for the promise of Isaiah 54:17. He did not allow any weapon to prosper against us, or any lying judgement to harm us, because our motives for service before God were pure. Our lives were spared, and our marriage has lasted twenty years.

My father's teeth

One memorable night in 1987 we at Namirembe Christian Fellowship held an all-night prayer meeting. These occasions were something of a preaching Olympics for me, as I would speak at midnight, having also been preaching for most of the day before. That night a large crowd had come together to praise, worship and pray. The noise was so great we virtually raised the roof. The blizzard of criticism was so strong at that time that we felt as if the Fellowship would be blown apart by it, or indeed the ground we were standing on collapse under the weight of it. When a miracle occurs it always stirs up controversy. Miracles so annoy Satan that he tries to sow confusion and criticism. Jesus also stirs people up in times of revival so that people are forced to take notice and decide either to oppose and curse, or to stand for God's glory.

My father, then aged seventy-three, had been especially moved by my sermon on the subject of Jesus' bones not being broken. Prophesied in Psalm 34:20, God protected the body of Jesus from having any bones broken when Jesus was not in a position to prevent this. It was normal practice for Roman soldiers to break the limbs of crucifixion victims to hasten their death. I drew a parallel with the defenceless believers under the cruel dictatorial regimes of those days in our country. I declared that they would be spared from the scary sporadic shootings if they would turn to Jesus and believe. As I returned to my chair, I was startled to see a word written on the seat in beautiful cursive letters, the word 'grazie'. I do not speak Italian, but I have a friend who knows a little. He said he thought it was Italian for 'thank you'. It was as if Jesus Himself had been right there and had written this as a special encouragement to me. Perhaps it was even the handwriting of that Someone who had stooped down to write in the Jerusalem dust before pronouncing judgement on the woman caught in adultery wrote with. It might have been an angel who wrote the message. I'm not making any special claims, but I know it was as if Jesus Himself was giving me confirmation that my bold declaration had His express approval.

My father however had not found my words an encouragement. 'If none of Jesus' bones were broken, how come God has not protected my teeth?' He had given his heart to the Lord some fourteen years before I was born and followed Him faithfully since then. 'All my life I have been waiting to see the God of miracles once more,' he said. This was his way of saying that he now had strong belief for a new set of teeth since he now only had a few teeth left. I laid hands on his jaw and said, 'Because you believe, you are going to see a miracle.' A week later my father was growing new teeth. He took out his false ones, cleaned them, and handed them to Celia as a souvenir. That is a good example of my assertion that God who created in the first place has not stopped the process. He has the power to polish up, rejig, recreate, call it what you like. Nature can be subjected to the will of God in a very amazing way. I emphasise, we believe in a God who can alter the very process of nature. Cancers, viruses, bacteria, parasites, wars, fractures, all can be reversed as we have seen.

A doctor healed of leukaemia

Dr Joachim Kiyimba now heads up a medical clinic run by the Orthodox Church in Uganda and also works as a general practitioner in Mulago Hospital. He came to see me in 1984, when he was very ill. He told me he had been diagnosed as suffering from leukaemia, a form of blood cancer, by the Mulago Hospital in Uganda, and had a second opinion confirming the diagnosis from the Jomo Kenyatta Hospital in Kenya. He said he knew he was going to die, but had come to see me at the request of his family who had agreed he should consult me in order to prepare himself for dying. I sensed there was a real World War going on in his mind, when I suggested that I should rather pray for his healing. He had redefined certain illnesses in retrospect as PUO (pyrexia of unknown origin), after some of his patients had been healed, to avoid the conclusion that God was involved. I shared my testimony, how I had as a young man had to turn away from my sinful way of life and that is was God's presence with me that prevented me from returning to my earlier way of life, such as partying, clubbing, drinking and so on which would condemn me to a Christ-less eternity. Finally he agreed to let me pray for him to be free of his disease. I advised him to return for further investigation to the original hospitals. Both said they could find no evidence of leukaemia. This was in spite of his having been hospitalised for eight months before he came to see me, and his having no chemotherapy whatsoever. Dr Kiyimba is now a firm believer in God's healing power. When he first told his colleagues that he had become a Christian and had been healed, they were of course sceptical. Some even called him crazy. I looked up the word crazy in a dictionary. Some alternatives would be foolish, mad, not sensible. Well, if that is what his fellow doctors meant, the truth is plain to see. Whereas in 1984 he had been on the verge of death, when I last saw him in 2000, he was at work, a well man. Beware of labelling something crazy just because you don't understand it.

There are times when we get a glimpse of a reality we had not previously been aware of. The Greek term for this revealing of alternative reality is the word *apocalypsis*. Faith in Jesus does just that; it reveals an alternative reality. Faith in Jesus enables Gentiles to come into the blessings promised by God to His chosen people Israel, not as substitutes, but as joint beneficiaries of His goodness. The meeting of Jesus with the Canaanite woman in Matthew 15:25–28 demonstrates this point rather well. She came to Jesus with her request and Jesus replied, *'It is not good to take the children's bread and throw it to the little dogs'* (v. 26). But that non-Jewish lady did not take offence, but persisted in pleading for the Jewish bread. Jesus acknowledged her faith and exclaimed, *' "O woman, great is your faith! Let it be to you as you desire." And her daughter was healed from that very hour'* (v. 28).

The faith that pleases God is that which acknowledges that we serve a God who does the impossible. When you come into those faith-stretching times of life, it is at that moment you encounter the miraculous intervention of God.

During the days of civil unrest after the overthrow of Idi Amin, the Namirembe Christian Fellowship met in a flimsy compound surrounded by papyrus reed fencing. It was certainly not the strength of building materials and design of fortification that led so many people to shelter with us for security. I often did not know how I was going to feed everyone. Even the water supply was uncertain. Local militia would often shoot at those who went to the wells to replenish supplies and as for running water out of a tap, that sophistication of infrastructure had long since been sabotaged. Every day some Good Samaritans would volunteer to risk their lives

to fill a few jerricans. It was a source of wonder that people
would leave their sturdy brick homes to huddle together in
our altogether more ramshackle accommodation.

There were around four hundred and fifty of us living in
these conditions. We had at one time only a meagre supply of
fish, which was past its best and well on the way to rotting,
and a quantity of old, stale maize which I was extremely
grateful for, supplied by the local Anglican Bishop. Many of
the children had diarrhoea. We had no medicines, no hospital
or medical help available. We had to look to God for healing
as the only recourse left to us. What was needed was not sweet
words from the preacher, but the hand of God demonstrating
the power of His will. The whole of Uganda was overcome
daily by what you may call 'the gates of hell'. It would look as
though God had totally abandoned our country to the worst
excesses of evil. Buildings were on fire all over the city,
resembling the very appearance of hell itself. The rule of the
gun was supreme. Any right-thinking person was incensed
with anger at the wanton destruction forced on us by ignorant
soldiery working out their frustration on other people's
property, all so a few vain men could exert their authority
and call themselves Head of State.

One afternoon I went to see how people in the Fellowship
Hall were coping with the rotten fish, the mouldy maize flour,
an army of mosquitoes, the sleepless nights from lack of
bedding and noise of gunfire. Though I thought the meagre
food and lack of facilities very poor hospitality, these people
were amazingly grateful for this level of luxury. Tears flowed
freely in that place, mine too, as I looked at this sorrowing
group of people God had entrusted to my care. I met the eye of
one mother. Her child had not eaten for thirty hours. The
water we had allocated for washing she regarded as too
precious to use for this purpose. She had boiled it in a small
saucepan and was giving it to her baby for lunch. We both
could not bear the pain in each other's eyes and looked away

quickly. Those eyes seemed to tear at me with such intensity; they reached through space as a direct prayer to the Almighty. I went outside to pray.

With such urgency my prayer went something like this, 'Do not expect me to wait, O Lord. I am not knocking at Your gates and waiting for permission to speak. I'm sorry; I have to burst in to tell You of these ordeals of mine.'

I heard Jesus speak to the innermost part of my heart. I was rooted to the spot, unable to move. I didn't stop to analyse whether it made sense or not. I knew it was the voice of Jesus using His authority to loose a blessing over His suffering people. The voice was shaking and breaking the foundation of the gates of hell. It was the voice of He who is the A to Z of life, the beginning of history, the Master of the future, even of Uganda's future. I prayed on.

'Stop praying, speak to the mango tree,' He commanded me.

There was a large mango tree, owned by my neighbour, just outside the compound, which hardly ever fruits. We had not seen any crop from it in years, and even later since things have settled down it has again reverted to a purely decorative state. My neighbour pruned it recently, so it is not nearly so impressive a sight, I really should have taken a photograph of it then to show you. What remains is on the cover of the book for you to see. Many people who have heard the story come on pilgrimage to see the famous tree. Anyway, I spoke to the tree, 'Listen to the Word of God, produce mangoes!' I declared. You would have thought I was a little mad if you could have heard me at that moment talking to a tree like this. There is a kind of madness that one may call keys to the heavenly kingdom, a boldness that might appear madness, but which is adorned with the beauty of faith and authority. It is not the madness of the madman of Gadara that binds the mind and soul in a prison of shame and nakedness; not the madness of demons inhabiting a body in their legions; not the oppression that causes a man to live stark naked among tombs in a graveyard, to scream at passers-by, so strong that no chains could contain him. This was the derangement of someone in touch with angels, indwelt by the Holy Spirit, 'endued with power', the upsurge of a throbbing voice of command and life that originates from Christ dwelling within. The power of Jesus that crushes the power of Satan frees people in bondage and causes nature to bow before its Creator. Like a woman who has given birth but who has not yet seen her child, I raised my hands in worship in spite of all the circumstances surrounding me at that moment, the turmoil in the country, the responsibility for feeding all these fugitives. There was not a mango in sight at that moment, but I was praising God for mangoes as if they were a reality you could touch or feel. We live by faith and not by sight.

A week later the tree was covered in white flowers. It was as if the tree had heard my words and was smiling encouragement at me. Another week and there was ripe fruit. My hungry people ate and ate. It fruited regularly until the war ended in 1986. It has not fruited since! Whenever I return from a speaking trip in other countries I love to spend a short time looking at the mango tree and remembering God's miraculous provision for us. It stands as a silent witness to God's love from that day to this.

Chapter 10

More Miracles of Healing

I have a photograph of a lively American brunette in my album. She is called Keren Allan. Keren works in a children's hospital in Mishiwaka, Indiana, USA. In 1997 Keren's sister Lisa called me in Uganda from the States to tell me that Keren was due to have an operation for kidney stones in three days time and would we pray for her. There obviously was not time for me to travel all the way to lay hands on Keren and pray for her in person, and in any case Keren and Lisa were not asking me to do this. What they wanted was for me to ask Jesus to let her join Him in His work of healing the sick, so Keren would not need the operation. I agreed and asked Lisa to lay her hand on the phone just as I was doing the other end. I heard from them later that surgery had not been needed after all. When she went to see the doctor on the third day, he had said she should carry on doing whatever she had done, since it had worked. 'I wish I had met Jesus before I spent so much money, many thousands of dollars, on my loathsome disease!' she said.

Why do people from the West, so advanced in many ways, need to hear testimonies of what God is doing in Africa? I believe it is because many of them give very clear insight into the ways Satan uses occult involvement to oppress people. The stories of deliverance that result from Jesus' work in our lives makes that aspect of Christ's redemption obvious when similar mechanisms are operating in more subtle ways in the context of Western society.

In the Bible we read many accounts of Jesus healing people through the casting out of demons. Jesus deliberately used to shock the Pharisees by kicking out demons, addressing Satan as an intelligent, sentient being who could respond to direct words of command. He clearly demonstrated the devil to be a living, active and malevolent personal entity, not just an impersonal evil force. The Bible is a narrative of actual deeds, not just a doctrinal or theological statement. The events really happened, and deep truth about God, man, and the future are clearly written for us to study and learn. The actual supernatural God we find in the Bible is the same One we worship today. We need to model our faith and action on Jesus' example so that we will not be weak or incompetent. The scribes give us a good example of people who teach, but their presentation is words only, not works as well as talk. The religious leaders of Jesus' day created a mighty edifice of rules, a ridiculous, impersonal religion, a strange, Godless righteousness. Jesus called them *'whitewashed tombs which indeed appear beautiful outwardly, but inside are full of dead men's bones and all uncleanness'* (Matthew 23:27).

Mark 1:22 says,

> *'And they were astonished at His teaching, for He taught them as one having authority, and not as the scribes.'*

Christianity is an astonishing teaching, different from the teachings of other wise men such as Socrates or Mohammed, or any other teacher the world may throw up. That is why we need the Holy Spirit. Without Him, living the Christian walk would be impossible. Jesus Himself, whose perfection was absolute, exceeding ours in every way imaginable, taught us that the power of the Holy Spirit is essential in our lives. The reason the Holy Spirit's presence is essential for us is that there is another spirit already dangerously infiltrating our lives.

*'Now there was a man in their synagogue with an unclean
spirit. And he cried out, saying, "Let us alone! What have we
to do with You, Jesus of Nazareth? Did You come to destroy
us? I know who You are – the Holy One of God!" But Jesus
rebuked him, saying, "Be quiet, and come out of him!" And
when the unclean spirit had convulsed him and cried out with
a loud voice, he came out of him. Then they were all amazed,
so that they questioned among themselves, saying, "What is
this? What new doctrine is this? For with authority He
commands even the unclean spirits, and they obey Him."'*

(Mark 1:23–27)

Jesus' teaching was an entirely new doctrine. Jesus' doctrine is
what Christianity is supposed to be today. Casting out
demons was a major part of Jesus' ministry when He walked
on the earth. See also Mark 1:39:

*'He was preaching in their synagogues throughout all Galilee,
and casting out demons.'*

Demons know Jesus. They also know us. Mark 1:34 says,

*'Then He healed many who were sick with various diseases,
and cast out many demons; And He did not allow the demons
to speak, because they knew Him.'*

In Mark 6:12–13, Jesus' followers were given power to cast out
demons, not only Jesus Himself. This ministry has been given
to believers to perform.

*'So they went out and preached that people should repent. And
they cast out many demons and anointed with oil many who
were sick, and healed them.'*

In court circumstantial evidence alone is not sufficient to
secure a conviction. But if circumstantial evidence is backed
by other evidence making a clear association between the

crime and the alleged suspect, then overwhelming evidence validates the circumstantial evidence. Christianity has to face the need for incontrovertible evidence of the message it proclaims. If the victory is won for us in Christ, then the Church should proffer hard evidence of their victorious life. I hope I have offered in these stories of my experience enough evidence of the unseen battle going on behind the scenes and of our victory over the forces of the devil. Too many people lead their lives in ignorance of this struggle so are not equipped to resist his power. Instead they are asleep when vigilance would be more appropriate. When indifference to Satan's devices reigns in the Church, they can be ambushed by such wickedness that they are in serious trouble before they realise it. Before the Church begins to take action, the world is tied up in any manner of satanically inspired wickedness that it is a monumental task to try and turn the tables on the enemy. However, if we have a true and firm connection with Christ, we can and will defeat Satan.

I remember one day in the eighties waiting in a queue to buy aspirin at a pharmacy. Out of nowhere this man attacked me verbally, saying, in Ugandan, 'Musajja, ggwe essaalazo zinnyonoona!' I could translate this for you, 'Hey you guy! Watch out, your prayers damn me!' I could feel there were demons in him, which were strongly objecting to my proximity. They did not like my relationship with Jesus one little bit. People standing near me turned to see what was happening. It does not surprise me in the least that some intellectuals with fine minds who are blind to their spiritual deception can argue cogently in opposition to the mind of Christ. Some will deliberately unite with Satan in fighting against God, others will be unaware how they are being used to add their weight to the wrong side.

I don't think we need more scientific or technological advances to unmask satanic deception. We share our bed with the ugly creature who burgles our house from day to day and who is bent on destroying us. Satan wants us to forfeit our inheritance and put our trust in the perishable things of earth. This way we end up with eternal regret. This is no mere cliché, I believe what I have witnessed is true. I am not saying believers never get ill, or die. Of course all of us are mortal. But I do say we should not give ground to the enemy to attack us with illness by continuing to live in sinful habits. If we do not drive Satan and his devious suggestions away from us, then we will end up jumping into bed with our arch-enemy. Indeed you may find yourself in hospital in the company of others who have allowed similar access to their bodies, supposed to be temples of the Holy Spirit. Satan has a field day walking up and down causing any manner of un-authorised misery and mayhem because believers allow just that. Against those unauthorised attacks God has appointed the Church to demonstrate His authority.

I am determined to play my part in warning as many as possible to save themselves, so that when the final resurrection comes I may acquit myself as worthy of my call. I hope that when I am gone, this testimony may still continue to give evidence for the truth that Jesus is Lord, and all authority on heaven and earth belongs to Him. I want to encourage those who have experienced the grief of losing a loved one to Satan's shameful tactics that they will one day enjoy the sight of Jesus' final overthrow of evil.

> *'And He will destroy on this mountain*
> *The surface of the covering cast over the people,*
> *And the veil that is spread over all nations.*
> *He will swallow up death forever,*
> *And the Lord GOD will wipe away tears*
>   *from all faces;*
> *The rebuke of His people*
> *He will take away from all the earth;*
> *For the LORD has spoken.'*   (Isaiah 25:7–8)

'O Death, where is your sting?
O Hades, where is your victory?'   (1 Corinthians 15:55)

Let me tell you another story of one of the members of the Namirembe Christian Fellowship. Mary Lubega's family lives in the village of Najjanankumbi, about a quarter of a mile away from the church. Mary married a Muslim businessman and converted to Islam. I was going to the missionary hospital in the village of Kayiwa near to where the Namirembe Christian Fellowship building is also situated, to pray for my friend Amos Ssempa, who was critically ill. In spite of our efforts to counteract evil forces, Amos's wife having told me of some unusual circumstances to do with his illness, his illness steadily progressed and he died. Mrs Ssempa wept. 'Couldn't Jesus do a miracle for us even at this stage?' she asked. I was leaving the hospital heartbroken and angry. I heard my name called, and was none too pleased to be interrupted in my grief.

I had no choice as a group of young men and women walked towards me so fast they had no difficulty in catching up with me, and calling out my name. They asked me to go and see the person in the room next door to where my friend was lying, who was Mary. She was totally blind and there was nothing medically that could improve her sight. Her daughter, a qualified nurse and on the staff of the hospital, was visiting. She had never seen anyone healed so put up firm resistance to my attempts to persuade her mother that improvement was possible. Satan also had a go at me. 'Who do you think you are,' he insinuated sneakily, 'Hasn't your friend just died in the room next door?' I made the effort to swim through the sea of doubt, reached shore and went ahead with my decision to pray for Mary – a Muslim, wealthy but lost.

I prayed three times without seeing any change. Then the Holy Spirit said to me, 'Don't pray any more, just order the spirit causing the blindness to go.' Her sight was restored immediately. Mary's daughter, the nurse, was beside herself with excitement. 'I have worked in this hospital for seven years. Never before have I seen such a thing as this.'

Mary got out of bed and went all round the hospital telling everyone what had happened. Without knowing it, she was giving a powerful boost to faith in Jesus in the place. After this I went through the whole hospital laying my hands on the other patients. Amazingly everyone was healed! Mary's Muslim husband was so pleased he threw a party to celebrate. Some time later I saw Mary at the wedding of Mary's niece, a mutual acquaintance. Mary rushed up to us and fell down at our feet worshipping God. Her sight has remained good since 1985.

In March 2000 I had another encounter with the heavenly realm. The tall angel I had met previously came and I knew I was in for another extraordinary experience. 'Where are we going?' I asked him. 'Are you afraid of leaving your body?' he replied with a question of his own. 'No, but I want to make sure that I live in the right place in eternity,' I replied.

'Where?' asked the angel.

'With my friend Jesus.'

At that he removed what looked to me like a cream-coloured sugar bowl from my chest and slid it down into my stomach. Perhaps it caused a temporary dysfunction of the heart. I still do not know whether I was really alive or dead at that point. I guess those who die are not aware of the moment's actual happening so it's nothing to get anxious about. I have had so many of these out of the body trips, it no longer concerns me at all. So don't worry about what is happening to Christians after death. Of course you will miss them and grieve, but what they are experiencing is not the message their decaying remains are giving you.

Immediately we flew away and having crossed the universe, entered heaven by the same gate already written about in the story of Ben. I saw again the incredible beauty of heaven. I had the familiar sensation of enjoyment of life, of the unspeakable fullness of everything. I felt myself blown through like a storm at sea, purified through and through, purged of envy, greed, violence mistrust, and spiritual apathy, cleansed from all those emotions that eat out the very heart of the people of the nations of earth. Earthly things became once again dull, boring, dark and oppressed, rulers all thirsty for power and covetous of wealth. I noticed a different perspective on the state of preachers. There were some screaming preachers longing for the Second Coming. Others' message, although proclaimed by well-known names, was obscured by the pride that blocked their vision.

The angel and I walked together over a magnificent, glittering glass floor, lit from below by a glorious flood of light. We shared our glee at being in this life, sweeter by far than any earthly joy. I found myself dressed in smart casual wear. My shoes were of a transparent glassy material which had the property of grasping the ground securely as I walked. These shoes gave me a new sense of authority, as if I had acquired with them greater authority over earthly spheres. My feet were not uncomfortable in these shoes. They caressed my feet like baby lotion and were flexible as I stepped out. I felt like the son of a wealthy chief in the homestead, carefully given every benefit money and position could offer.

We saw a group of over fifty happy children. As we passed they turned their joyful faces to look at us with radiant smiles. Although no words passed between us, our hearts communicated a sense of their pleasure at being allowed to see someone from earth. These were children who had been born, but who died while still very young so had no memory of what life on earth was like. They were eagerly waiting for the promise of a return when Jesus comes back to reign. They were very excited as they eagerly waited for Jesus to descend once again to the earth. If I could describe them, they resembled young people of between eight and seventeen years old. No trace of doubt was in their minds, they were destined to rule for ever with the King of kings.

Eventually I returned to my body. By this time I was familiar with the process. I started connecting at the head and the conversation with the angel continued until I was fully back, seated on the bed looking at the place where the angel had been sitting talking to me. I knew I was once more assigned a task for my time on earth. While I was in heaven, I received another message to tell the people of Uganda. We would go through another period of stress. If we worship and trust Him, He will help us go safely through our hardships. He also said I was to travel round the world.

I shared this revelation with Celia and later with the church and with an American couple, Cheryl and Rocky from Idaho Christian Fellowship which was started as a daughter church of Namirembe Christian Fellowship. Only a month later we had a spectacular tragedy. A thousand people lost their lives when a cult leader murdered them. Born-again churches were blamed for this disaster. Once again denominational differences became sharply divided, the Anglican, Roman Catholic and Orthodox churches sided with the government against those of the born-again persuasion. In the end this disaster formed the foundation for greater unity among all the churches as we strove to put in place agreements to prevent a similar cultic tragedy being able to occur.

Chapter 11

Believe God for a Miracle

As I conclude this book, I would just recap on what we have
learned. First I know that heaven exists. It is a real place you
have the opportunity of reaching. Secondly there is an intense
battle going on to prevent you from reaching this desired
destination. I am not the inventor of God. Please don't shoot
the messenger; I'm not trying to disturb you in any way, or to
coerce you in any way that would deprive you of your freewill
choice. I don't seek status or recognition. Those of you who
have heard me will understand my sincerity when I state this.
I have the problem of communicating the unique events I
have truly experienced. If you think I am deceived, then ask
those people who have been healed since I showed them
my God.

I know from my own experience that knowing about God is
not the same thing as knowing God. The Name of Jesus is well
known. Jesus is a celebrity, you might say. And like all celebrities He has many people who know a great deal about Him
without having been personally introduced. Indeed, many
people would be conversant with a great deal of theological
argument, religious observance and understanding of Church
tradition without a personal relationship with the Saviour
Himself. There is no substitute for the indwelling presence
of God in a believer, not ceremonial, clothing, religious
observance, lighting candles, olive oil, long beards etc. We
have all heard of famous actors, presidents of countries,

153

astronauts, reigning monarchs and royal families etc., but do we really know them? Even if we were to talk in great detail about them, if we were to meet them we would still need an introduction.

The intention behind this book is that you may have a personal introduction to the living God, who saves, delivers and heals today, just the same as we read about in the New Testament. It is perfectly possible for you to read this book and to receive a miracle. Like the woman who touched Jesus' garment and was healed of a haemorrhage which had rendered her unclean for many years, you can be free of oppression even if you have been oppressed for a long time. The greatest miracle is always freedom from the consequences of your own sin. This one problem is the only one that can separate you from the joys of heaven I have described to you. All the things you could have in Jesus you might miss if you thought I am trying to deceive you.

Jesus taught His disciples a great many important things in the meal just before He went to the cross. In John 14:19–21 He said,

> '*A little while longer and the world will see Me no more, but you will see Me. Because I live, you will live also. At that day you will know that I am in My Father, and you in Me and I in you. He who has My commandments and keeps them, it is he who loves Me. And he who loves Me will be loved by My Father, and I will love him and manifest Myself to him.*'

The part I want to emphasise from these verses is the promise that Jesus will manifest Himself, introduce Himself, and make Himself obvious. The manifestation of God's presence is the miracle Jesus wants you to experience. Whether you need to turn from things you feel offend your conscience but you find it hard to stop, or whether you need healing from the hurts of the past, or physical healing for an illness, when you believe, all things become possible. If you have a condition the experts have declared there is no known solution for, such as an incurable illness, you may find it very difficult not to be so weakened in spirit that prayer seems meaningless. I understand how that feels, as I was in that state before Jesus met me that day in the teacher's sitting room. It is important that you don't go and do something foolish at that moment which might aggravate the situation. I have heard of people turning to witchdoctors and other occult activities in their desperation. Others have attempted suicide, or have turned against God, blaming Him for their predicament. My story is that Jesus met me and sent me to tell others. It was clear to me that these were the very people He had in mind for me to find and tell this message, 'Tell the world, I am the greatest power in heaven and earth.' He will free us from all bondage if we believe.

The story of the healing of the decaying body of a man with leprosy in Matthew 8 always has special meaning for me. I identify with his story as one who also suffered from a stigmatising condition, which ostracised me from polite society, was not life threatening but extremely debilitating in its cruelty and the effect of the trauma and mental pain it caused me. I too was a man of no social worth. My woman-ising, drunken and evasive lifestyle caused me to be on the brink of disaster. Such a one was not likely to hear from God. Ritually unclean, the leper would be subject to loss of family, paid employment and home. The priest would declare him separated from God, doomed to be cut off from the congregation of Israel and isolated from his family. From the moment of diagnosis, the sufferer was forced to maintain his own separation by carrying a bell and calling out, 'Unclean!' Even a king was subject to the same condition, forced to relinquish the throne and be subject to quarantine. If he appeared near anyone, a crowd would scream and curse him to drive him away. There was no known cure, unlike today when there is effective treatment, so great deformity would develop so the person became progressively more repulsive, his clothes poor and tattered. He smelt from open wounds, his hands shrunken to twisted stubs, numb, paralysed and useless, his feet bleeding and insensitive, his nose disappeared, his eyes blinded through lack of ability to blink.

It was such a person who one day heard of Jesus and took the decision to go and find Him. In spite of the hostile crowd, this man pursued Jesus until he was right next to Him, the crowd recoiling in fear lest they too became contaminated. The horrid spectacle of the man not even six feet away, but lying prostrate at Jesus' feet worshipping Him, completely contradicted convention. No-one had been healed before of this disease. Naaman's healing was way in the past and long since forgotten. Such a thing was unheard of at that time. The leper's faith was not based on the opinions of the crowd, but on his own perception of Jesus. Acting on his own revolutionary faith he asked something of Jesus that had not been done before. He was aware of the rules of society, but also that Jesus would not turn anyone away who came to Him for help. So he demonstrated his understanding of the nature of God and worshipped Him. His faith was not based on human wisdom, but on foolishness, impudence, impoliteness and immodesty as he lay before his Lord. He may have had a weak, foul-smelling body, but he had a strong, courageous inner man. He was able to stand on the promise of God, impious, risky and illegal, as it seemed.

Perhaps Jesus was reminded of His own suffering yet to come as He looked down on this poor wretch. I wonder if the words of Isaiah 1:5–6 went through His mind:

> '*Why should you be stricken again?*
> *You will revolt* [sin] *more and more.*
> *The whole head is sick,*
> *And the whole heart faints.*

> *From the sole of the foot even to the head,*
> *There is no soundness in it,*
> *But wounds and bruises and putrefying sores;*
> *They have not been closed or bound up,*
> *Or soothed with ointment.'*

In other words, when you are so sick, my friend, why should you be cursed again? Your suffering needs to be healed, not made worse with added insult.

> *' "Come now, and let us reason together,"*
> *Says the* LORD,
> *Though your sins are like scarlet,*
> *They shall be as white as snow;*
> *Though they are red like crimson,*
> *They shall be as wool.*
> *If you are willing and obedient,*
> *You shall eat the good of the land.'*   (Isaiah 1:18–19)

Don't be talked out of expecting God to move on your behalf by your friends or by a perception of God as weak because of your religious background. You need to forget the weak impression of God that has dwelt in your mind since you were young. Jesus was not afraid of ritual uncleanness or of getting the disease. He deliberately reached out and touched this man, in all his condition. Far from Jesus becoming unclean, an amazing thing happened. All evidence of the leprosy left the man, the unclean cleansed by an encounter with God.

Remember Sarah, Abraham's wife who asked, *'How can this be?'* when the angel informed her she would have a son (Genesis 18:10) at her age, when she was over eighty. It can still be if you believe. Though it may look impossible to man, with God all things are possible. Moses said, 'send someone else', when God asked him to lead the Children of Israel out of slavery, but God insisted on sending fearful, shy, stammering

Moses all the same. Zechariah's wife was promised a son whose name would be John. She too was an old lady. She became pregnant all the same and John was born.

I have forgotten the number of times I have had someone laugh incredulously when I have given them a word from God. Mary said to the angel *'How can this be, since I know no man?'* But she conceived all the same. When God has promised something, we had better drop our natural reactions. I commend to you the God of miracles, even if you may be a sinner. For everything is possible when you believe.

Let's pray,

> 'Jesus, I thank You for the many miracles I have seen and I ask now, that You meet the needs of this person who is reading this book. Meet them, Lord Jesus, as You promised with the manifestation of Your presence. Please forgive them of their sin as they reach out to You to believe that Your death and resurrection purchased their life from the fiery eternity and give them a glimpse of heaven. If their body is sick, please heal them, if their mind tormented by the hurts of the past, give them the ability to forgive their tormentor and receive new life in You, Jesus.
> **Amen.**'

If you have any questions or requests to make, please
contact us at:

Namirembe Christian Fellowship
PO Box 9096
Kampala
Uganda

Tel/Fax: 041-256-273441

Mobile: 077503654
077423231
077509283

email: kayiwa2@yahoo.com